AF701047

NOBODY'S GONNA DIE TODAY

NOBODY'S GONNA DIE TODAY

The Story of the LSU Player Who Was Shot By a Dog

MATT BRANCH AND LIANA BRANCH

WESTMINSTER
Publishing House

Nobody's Gonna Die Today
The Story of the LSU Player Who Was Shot By a Dog

ISBN-13:
979-8-218-20172-2 Paperback
979-8-218-20173-9 Hardcover
LCCN: 2023908569

Westminster Publishing House
Monroe, Louisiana

Table of Contents

FORWARD

By: Tommy Moffitt

I hadn't heard from Matt in a while but wasn't surprised when he texted me. We managed to stay in touch after he left LSU and had spoken about the accident and his rehab on several occasions. I figured that his call had something to do with hunting season, the Tigers' upcoming bowl game against Purdue, or maybe even high school football.

I must be honest I was a little shocked when he told me that he had written a book. I was very familiar with his accident and all he had to overcome, but never took Matt as the literary type. I knew he had worked very hard to walk again and why, but I didn't know the whole story.

I've never been the type of person to pry or ask a lot of questions about a person's suffering, I consider them a private matter and a need-to-know basis. I figured if he wanted me to know, he would tell me. When he told me that he had written a book, his idea of the title and he wanted me to write the forward, I was speechless. I didn't know how to respond or what to say. I gave him the courtesy of a, "wow, thanks man, that means a lot to me" kind of a reply, unsure of the right words to say.

It was a few days before Christmas when I got the manuscript for the book. The annual whitetail deer rut was starting to heat up around home, and we had holiday plans to visit family and friends in New Orleans. Like many this time of the year, I was thinking about how blessed we are to live the life that we do, and the birthday of our Lord and Savior, Jesus Christ. The reason we gather and celebrate Christmas.

Never in my wildest dreams did I believe I would spend the next four days glued to this story. I couldn't put it down for a single minute. With all that was going on around me, all I could do was focus on the story, the next sentence, the next chapter, anticipating what would happen.

I thought that I had suffered in my life, I thought that I knew how tough life could be, and what it took to fight and overcome adversity. Compared to what happened to Matt and everything he had to go through; I had no clue. The incredible thing about the book is how easy it was for Matt and Liana to put it into words, their words. How wonderfully they were able to remember, articulate and tell their story, is nothing short of a miracle.

Matt's story is riveting, awe-inspiring, scary, and even grotesque at times, but it's real. This isn't a fairy tale about a guy who has a successful college football career, then gets shot in the leg and lives to talk about it. This book is about rebellion, loss, tragedy, faith, family, inspiration, and love. It's a story about hard work, redemption, and second chances. A story about forgiveness, forgiving yourself, and being able to look at yourself in the mirror say you're sorry and do your best to love yourself for who you really are. Not someone you think you should be.

I hope that you get as much from this book as I did. It's hard to put into words how moving it can be. Fortunately for the readers, Matt, and Liana, did an amazing job at that and I know that you will be moved by them.

PROLOGUE

Suddenly I was awakened by the unpleasant feeling of being thrown back into my body! I could barely squint my eyes to gaze around the room. I heard people talking to me. It was Liana! How did she get here so fast, and why was she crying? I tried turning my head to look at her, but I couldn't.

I was paralyzed.

The room seemed cold, unsettling, and as if it was closing in on me. I could see that I was lying flat on a table or bed. "What was this?" I thought. "Where am I?" I had an object in my mouth and throat and could not speak. I tried to move my toes to give Liana a sign that I could hear her, but this was impossible. Then I tried blinking to show my wife a sign of life, but I didn't have the strength. I was struck with the thought that I may never move again and wanted to cry. My mind raced, and I felt maybe I was in hell. My thoughts and emotions bounced around the room while my body lay lifeless. I was terrified that my short life was over. Then as quickly as I had awoken, darkness fell back upon me.

My twelve-day fight for life had just begun.

Doctors, nurses, and paramedics exhausted themselves, trying everything imaginable to save me. Luckily, I do not remember anything after going into cardiac arrest. I fell into a twelve-day coma and had many bizarre, strange, and unnerving vivid dreams I remember in detail. I have dreams almost every night, but I can't remember them the way I remember my comatose dreams.

At times I wonder if they were even dreams. Could they have been visions of the afterlife? I can't rightly say. The strange nature of my dreams or visions was not necessarily biblical but disturbing. People I have known throughout my life were in them. "Could this have been a type of purgatory?" I wondered.

I was living out a life in these dreams. I believed they were a part of my life, and it took my family weeks to convince me that I had been lying motionless in a hospital bed the entire time. If I had never woken up, would I still be living in that chaotic reality today? Maybe this was nothing more than just dreams, and there was no meaning behind any of them. But maybe there was? This question will forever be on my mind.

CHAPTER 1
December 28, 2018

The old car horn of my phone alarm went off, and I cracked my eyes open. I had fallen asleep with the TV on watching my favorite comedy, The Office, so there was ample light to gaze around the 1990s-era decorated hunting camp bedroom. I rolled to my side and slid out from under the old floral-printed bed comforter. Both feet hit the navy-colored carpet at 5:45 on the morning of December 28, 2018. I had no idea this would be the last time both my feet would hit the floor for the rest of my life. I reached for my iPhone to check and see if I had any messages and take a quick look at the weather forecast. I rolled my eyes, seeing it would be a nasty wet day, and briefly considered getting back under that floral comforter. It was a fleeting thought.

The other guys in camp would not let me get away with this and had I tried, they would have made me more miserable than facing this day. Or so I thought. Against my wishes, I stood up and walked to the light switch by the door. Once the light removed the darkness, I grabbed my duffle bag and dug through it, determined to find the perfect outfit.

Although it's never discussed, hunters have a strong desire to be the best dressed in the blind. I picked out a solid tawny-colored plain long-sleeve shirt, Red Head brand khaki work pants, and a pair of patterned fuzzy warm wool socks. My outer ensemble would be a solid brown softshell jacket, which perfectly mismatched my pair of natural gear banded waders. Meryl Streep would be proud.

The temperature was supposed to start in the high forties, then climb to the mid-fifties by lunch. Once I got my perfect outfit just right, I headed down the short hall for the camp kitchen.

My first stop was the Keurig in the corner. Coffee is a necessity for the avid duck hunter. I crave the taste of a hot cup of dark brew in the blind before sunrise almost more than I crave ducks landing the decoys. However, I would not be in a blind that morning. I had to quickly enjoy my delicious black coffee at camp.

The aroma of fresh coffee mixed with two-day-old dirty dishes began to circulate through the camp, and one by one, the other proud sportsmen poked their heads out of their bedrooms. Each man performed his morning ritual. Some of these rituals are best left unsaid.

No one was bursting with excitement. Everyone saw the weather would be awful, and we all knew the hunting would likely be the same.

This hole is not what I would call consistent. Sometimes it's a bang, and sometimes it's a bust, which is typical for most duck holes in the south these days.

Most of the time, it seems far more often, the act of waking up early and wading through the mud and muck is a wasted effort. However, addictions are hard to stop. Each one of us considered ourselves a great duck hunter, and nobody was willing to ruin their reputation.

We pow-wowed in the kitchen and confirmed our plan to split up and hunt in small groups. I was going solo that morning. We found a new spot, and there were few places to hide. We glassed quite a few birds in this spot the day prior and didn't want to ruin it by adding too many bodies to the limited natural cover.

As I stepped out onto the newly remodeled wooden porch, the strong scent of fresh mud after heavy rain invaded my nostrils. Ah, what a pleasure to be a duck hunter. It was indeed a painfully sloppy day, and we would have to work to shoot a limit. I took a couple of steps across the cherry stained two by fours to where my waders, which had seen better days, were hanging.

December 28, 2018

Waders are a necessary evil when duck hunting at Eagle Lake. They are no fun to put on and wear, but unless you enjoy getting as muddy as a barn animal, you better have a pair.

I slid my feet into the boots and pulled the waterproof upper to my chest. I tried to snap the belt and grunted, realizing I had to let it out a touch. "Guess the burgers and beer last night didn't do my waistline any favors," I thought. After that, I skipped down the brick stairs while humming "Tuesdays Gone" by Lynyrd Skynyrd and beelined to my truck across the camp yard. The coffee was working.

I recited the list of necessities in my head, "gun, calls, shells, decoys, bucket, gun case." I opened the back door of my Ford F-150 and started sorting through the junk.

My back seat is always a wreck that time of year. For me, this is when hunting and selling season coincide. I have everything necessary to sell a pallet of cottonseed and bag a limit of ducks all before lunch.

The weather was similarly nasty the morning prior, so after yesterday's hunt, I pulled my shotgun out of the case so rust would not build up on it. I loved my twelve-gauge Beretta A390. My dad bought me this shotgun on my eighteenth birthday. I had gotten his money's worth over the last eleven seasons, and I knew the story behind every nick and scratch. I had grown to love how the gun shouldered to me, and I was confident in taking any shot with it. When I shouldered it, it felt like an extension of myself. I had brought down several limits with it, and I was hoping to bring down one more that morning.

My old Beretta did not have a cerakote finish, so meticulous care was needed to keep it in peak form. I grabbed the shoulder strap to retrieve my gun because it would take the least effort to reach. As I fished it up from the explosion of junk it was buried under, something I didn't expect happened. The carry strap, which had been married to my Berretta for the past ten seasons, filed for divorce. A brief panic, followed by a mild annoyance, crashed my mood. I mumbled a few four-letter words and kicked the side of my truck, hoping my broken gun strap somehow noticed how upset I was. Since I would have nothing but water and flimsy coffee beans around me, I would have to dreadfully hold my gun the entire hunt. And because Beretta didn't care for convenience, any spare straps lying around the camp were useless. The A390 model requires a unique strap because it does not have a swivel stud on the end cap—uh, annoying.

I quickly moved on from my heartache and continued gathering my gear. It was time to move on from my unfaithful gun strap. After all, there were plenty of willing companions at Simmons Sporting Goods. I grabbed my camouflage gun case, fully expecting its deceit, but our bond remained strong. I carefully slid my Beretta down into it, hoping not to upset it in any way.

It was now time to load everything on my cousin's trusty Honda Rancher four-wheeler. I made sure he noticed the paint was starting to chip so he couldn't blame it on me later. After securing all my gear, I perched up on the leather seat. I glanced around and noticed I was the first one ready.

It is known among hunters that the first one ready gets the privilege of heckling everyone else for being slow. Personally, I love this tradition. I am famous for my natural talent for being a jackass. After my unwelcome bickering, the others finished loading up.

My cousin David Joe was driving a squatting-in-the-rear Polaris Ranger that was loaded down with four hunters, their gear, and a dog. I had the Honda Rancher all to myself. I asked him which way he thought I should drive into my hunting spot. I had two options: a muddy turn row through the farm or a smooth blacktop road.

He gave me a dumb look and said, "You're kidding, right?"

I said, "I just wanted to make sure you were thinking the same thing I was."

We then cranked up and pulled out of the ill-lit camp yard. As I pulled onto the road, it dawned on me that I had forgotten shotgun shells. The only thing worse than forgetting shells is forgetting your shotgun. Luckily, I hadn't gone far, so I turned around and headed back to my truck.

When I got within striking distance, I leaped off the Rancher while it was still rolling. I wanted to hurry so the others wouldn't see that I had forgotten something. The heckling would have been returned if they found out I had broken tradition. I emptied a box in my chest pocket, then grabbed two handfuls from another box and stuffed them into my jacket. I figured thirty-five-ish shells should be plenty for a crack shot like me to shoot a limit of six ducks. I shuffled back over to the Rancher that had barely come to a complete stop and hit the gas.

When I grabbed the handlebars, a thought came to me. Maybe the blacktop would be too dangerous at night. This was Eagle Lake, where the redneck yacht club originated. There was a solid chance I could encounter a drunk down on his luck after hitting the Vicksburg casino all night. Against my cousin's advice, I decided to change plans and go through the farm.

The freshly rained-on turn row was a muddy mess. Although great for growing corn, soybeans, and cotton in the spring and summer, the soil on the farm was a nightmare in the rainy winter months.

One December day in my teenage years, I borrowed my dad's Polaris Ranger to slip up on a big rack buck. The farm had received fresh rain on that day as well. As a result of the tires becoming utterly covered with mud, both front axles snapped. Because I was a broke teenager, my dad had to foot the bill. What I know now that I did not know then is that you must drive the tires through every water puddle you encounter. This keeps mud from building up to the point that the tires will no longer spin.

While driving down the turn row, I was challenged to a friendly game of what I call dodge the flying mud clod. This game is like dodgeball, except I was only allowed to dodge. Every so often, a mud clod would fly up in the air, thrown by one of the tires. If I successfully dodged the mud clod, I got the point. If the mud clod landed on me or any of my gear, the tires got the point. Let's just say the tires were setting a new high score that morning. I was starting to regret not taking the blacktop.

I cursed myself for changing my route at the last second, but I had already come too far to turn around. I started to wonder why I had changed my mind to go through the farm in the first place. The strange silence and stillness in the air made it feel almost like there was a sort of presence with me. Knowing what I know now, I can't help but think there was, in fact, someone watching over me that day.

As I came upon the first canal I had to cross, I slowed down a little. There were dozens of culverts spread throughout the farm, and I knew how to navigate each one of them. I had been crossing them on ATVs, trucks, and tractors since I was a kid. I was in no real hurry that morning; I had enough time to get set up before shooting hour. I eased over the culvert and turned left, heading east toward my hunting spot. The other group kept driving straight or south after the culvert. They would be setting up about a half-mile from me.

A couple of hundred yards later, I came upon a second culvert crossing. As I got close, I noticed that water was covering the road. This was not alarming. Large farm equipment crosses these culverts every day through the spring and summer, so they are built very wide and easy to navigate. I knew the water depth was only a couple of inches deep over the culvert crossing, but still, I slowed down to make sure I was centered. After all, the water depth on the sides of the culvert was deep enough to lose a truck in, so I wanted to minimize my chance of getting baptized in the cold muddy water. Falling into cold, icy water on a duck hunt is a close third on the list of things not to do right after forgetting your gun or shells.

I picked my mark and slowly pressed on the gas. Everything went smoothly at first. The subtle splashing of the tires moving through the water was a satisfying sound. When I made it halfway across, I noticed the water was a little deeper than I expected. I glanced up to check my course and realized something was wrong. I looked back down at the water when my right front tire suddenly took a nosedive. I panicked and punched the gas. My thought was if I kept the ATV moving, I could walk it to the other side. I slid my foot into the water, hoping to find the ground so I could keep the ATV from flipping on top of me. My leg was not long enough, and before I could think, the ATV flipped and landed on me, pinning me underwater. Luckily the water was deep enough so I could slide out from under the ATV. I released the handlebars and franticly splashed around like a toddlers first time in a swimming pool before making my way to dry ground.

I sloppily climbed out of the water, stood up, took a couple of deep breaths, and glanced back toward the submerged ATV in disbelief. I felt my eyes bulge from their sockets as I screamed a chain of four-letter words that would make a sailor blush. All my gear had fallen off the Honda and was now floating away down the canal in the dirty water. I shook my head in utter disbelief and shock.

Things like this don't happen to me. I never get in too big of a hurry and always play it on the safe side.

I am more conservation-minded when it comes to hunting than most. Old soul, I guess. People usually tease me because I don't always shoot when birds fly within range. Sometimes I like to just sit and watch as everybody else jumps to shoot at the flying winged marvels.

My philosophy on hunting has changed over the last few years. When I was younger, I always had big plans to travel the world and hunt every game animal this earth had to offer. But the older I have become; I have begun to learn to appreciate having the opportunity to enjoy the sport. I try not to get so caught up in wishing I had a better place to hunt. Instead, I try to enjoy the opportunities I have instead of always looking for the next great expensive adventure to go on.

Since I couldn't undo what had already been done, I attempted to salvage what I could of the situation. I carefully made my way back down the muddy bank into the water and gathered my gear. Once I had collected my belongings, I climbed out of the canal and checked over everything. My gun case had taken a bath underwater and was thoroughly soaked. I pulled my gun out of it and laid it on the ground. If I left it in the case, my beloved Beretta would have undoubtedly rusted over.

I had experienced a shocking wreck like this one other time in my life.

FLASHBACK

October 2008

Several of my teammates and I bought Yamaha Zuma 49cc mopeds our freshman year at LSU. We were cool. Plus, I got my money's worth of that scooter through college. I could sleep in at WCA up to five minutes before class, run downstairs, hop on my scooter, park at the front door of Locket Hall, and sit down before the teacher showed up. It also saved me a lot of steps around campus, which kept my legs fresh for practice and workouts. We had our own biker gang and treated campus as our home turf.

One day I rode my scooter around Mike's cage, and he started chasing me like I was a gazelle on the loose. The feeling of having a full-grown tiger chasing you is exhilarating, even if there was a thick glass wall separating us.

One day 88, 47 (I'll use jersey numbers here), and I were headed to practice after class. We were up to our usual antics, goofing off, taunting each other, and speeding through campus. As we rode down Victory Hill, I turned around and gave 47 the bird. His eyes suddenly doubled in size, and he started to mouth something. I whipped my head around and noticed 88, riding in front of me, had come to a complete stop. I panicked and squeezed the brakes. Naturally, the brake I mashed was for the front tire, and I went airborne.

I flipped over my handlebars and landed headfirst on the blacktop. The moped landed on top of me, and I began to slide down the asphalt. I had been going about 35 mph when this happened, so I ended up sliding over fifty feet down the road. My arms and legs were ripped to shreds, and my clothes were torn and tattered. Classes had just let out, so there was an abundance of witnesses if this accident ever went to court.

People dropped their books and jumped out of their cars, running over to see if I was alright. I was in complete shock at what had just happened. I stood up and wobbled around for a second, trying to gather myself. I picked up my scooter and sat back down on the seat. I looked down at my feet and noticed my

Crocs were missing. I curiously looked around, wondering how my shoes had fallen off. I turned left and spotted one Croc on the far side of the road. Then turned right and eyed my second Croc on the other side of the road. I dropped the kickstand on my moped, gathered my shoes, sat back on the seat, cranked up, and headed to practice.

When I got to Football Ops, I felt overwhelming nausea come over me. I looked at my knee, and I thought I could see the white bone of my kneecap. Luckily, 88 and 47 helped me walk into the training room, where I lay on a table and felt like I would throw up. I rolled to my side and puked my guts up for ten minutes.

Let's just say I didn't make it to practice that afternoon.

To this day, I still have a massive scar on my right knee to remind me never to flip people off while riding a moped.

CHAPTER 2
I Hate to Exercise

All that was left visible of the ATV were the handlebars and back rack. My financially driven mind started calculating how many bones this incident would set me back. "David Joe will never let me hear the end of this," I thought. After my Jedi mind trick did not lift it out of the water, I decided I would have to call for help. The brand-new Polaris Ranger had a winch that would pull the Rancher out in a flash.

I reached into my chest pocket to find my iPhone and came up empty-handed. My first thought was it was probably lying at the bottom of the canal. I desperately searched all my pockets and ah-ha! It was in my pants pocket. I had to squirm a little to slide my hand down inside my waders to fish it out. My pocket felt dry, so I thought my phone would be fine. I had owned a cell phone for fifteen years, and I had never lost or broken one. But on this day, my bad luck streak would continue. I hit the button to unlock my iPhone, but the screen stayed black. I angrily started smashing it, thinking it might turn on if it could feel my frustration. It never came around, and I added an iPhone to my list of things I had to pay to fix or replace.

I knew Liana was going to kill me. I'm not the best about backing my phone up, so there was no telling how many pictures of our son's birth had just vanished into thin air.

"What now?" I thought. I had no phone, ride, or ducks. By this time, daylight had come, and the other two groups had started shooting. They were shooting quite a lot, and I became frustrated that I wasn't joining in on the fun.

My thoughts turned back to the submerged ATV, and I tried to think of a way to get it out of the canal. I curiously looked around for anything that could aid me in this monumental task. All I could see was mud and water in every direction. The only thing I had to do for the job was muscle, and at that time in my life, I severely lacked in it. Weighing in at a solid 280 pounds in my birthday suit, my muscle was far outmatched by fat. Remarkably, I had managed to keep nearly all my football-playing weight while losing over half of the muscle of my former self. This was not an easy task. It required a disciplined regime, including an incredible number of Miller Lites and cheeseburgers. I knew I would have to dig down deep to not become nauseated from the strenuous redneck-style workout that lay before me.

Against my wishes, I marched back down in the canal. The water the rancher was in was close to five feet deep. This made it extremely hard to get leverage and build up any momentum.

I pushed and pulled for ten minutes and got nowhere. I became so winded that I had to take a break. I was so tired, midway up the bank, and I slipped and clumsily rolled back into the water. I didn't have the strength to stand back up, so I sunk my elbows in the mud and crawled up the soupy bank. When I sat down, I couldn't decide if I wanted to laugh or cry. This was my worst hunt in recent memory, and it wasn't even 7 a.m.

After I caught my breath, I started to look up in the sky for ducks. I noticed several groups flying the area, and I glanced over at my disappointed shotgun. I had just about given up on the submerged Honda. I was going to need help to get this thing out. I stood up and looked over my gear. "Wait," I thought. Where are my mojo decoys? It dawned on me that they were sitting under five feet of water and were likely ruined. Add another $300 to my tab for the day.

"This day just keeps getting better and better," I thought.

Instead of leaving the mojos for the fish to claim, I figured I would look for them. They were attached to the mud stakes, so I shouldn't have had to kick around long to find them. After about a minute of unenthusiastic kicking, I found them. I hooked one with my foot, reached down, and grabbed it with my hand. I then hooked the second one with my foot, reached down, and missed my grab. Another string of four-letter words echoed across the farm. I took a deep breath and hooked it again, reached down, and grabbed it—two mojos in hand, and I made my way back up the bank.

Since I went through the trouble of retrieving the mojos from the water, I might as well see if they still worked. They had been at the bottom of the canal for at least forty-five minutes. Battery-operated electronic spinning wing mojo decoys were not made to be underwater for that long, or at all for that matter. So, I was expecting them to need significant repairs. I clicked the button on the first one, nothing. I clicked the button on the second one, and holy cow! It worked! The wings were not spinning at full speed, but they were turning fast enough to possibly lure a mallard drake into shooting range. "Finally, good news today," I thought.

After finding out that one mojo worked, I got my second wind. I decided I would give it one more shot to push the ATV out of the water. I briefly looked around, hoping a wandering duck hunter, farmhand, or lost gambler from the highway to the casino might magically appear and offer help. After being reassured I was utterly alone, I bailed off back down in the canal.

I didn't have much hope, but after a couple of minutes, I finally started to make some progress. At the end of a ten-minute struggle, I managed to get the back tires onto dry ground. I was breathing so hard that I had to take a break, but if I let go, I feared all my progress would be lost. I leaned my shoulder into the front bumper and pushed against it as hard as I could. I felt like I had a solid hold, and I rested there in five feet of water with a 700-pound Honda propped up on my shoulder. I wish somebody would have been there to take a picture of that sight.

I caught my breath and went back to work. After another fifteen minutes of pushing and pulling, I managed to get the

Rancher out of the water. I crawled up the bank and laid down in the Mississippi mud. I couldn't remember any old football workout that had me breathing this heavily.

I mustered up what little energy I had left and walked over to the Rancher. I pulled the seat off and opened the airbox. It was full of water. I pulled the filter off and wrung it out to dry. Then I started draining the water out of the airbox. I have been a country boy all my life, and this was not the first ATV I had ever flooded out. After I decided I had done all I could without the proper equipment, I put all the parts back together and tried to crank it up. I turned the key and hit the starter, but nothing. I gave the Rancher a good shake, turned the key, hit the starter, and again, nothing. This thing wasn't even attempting to crank; it was time to move on.

I walked back over to where my gun was lying and sat down. For once, the weatherman was right. The sky was dark grey, and it looked as if it might start pouring rain any second.

Cloudy, rainy days are not suitable for duck hunting. When it's cloudy, ducks can see hunters trying to hide in the brush much better because there is no glare shining off the water or sun to act as a blinder. I started to run through my options in my head. I could sit here and wait on them to finish hunting, then try to catch their attention to come pick me up. This was a little risky. If I didn't get their attention, I would be stranded and must walk all the way back to camp. Option two was to walk down the foggy cypress brake to where they were hunting, so I would guarantee I would be picked up.

I checked my G-Shock, and it was a little after 8 a.m. Between the middle group of guys and me was a giant dead cypress tree. I had been on many good duck hunts standing under that old cypress. It is so large in diameter that it would take three people to stretch around the base. The texture of the bark is like driftwood that washes up on the beach. I realized that if I hurried, I still had time to get a little hunting in before everyone was ready to call it quits or move to another spot. I quickly decided I would go for option two, and I grabbed my shotgun and semi-working mojo and trudged off toward the old cypress tree.

I decided to not bring my shotgun case because it was soaking wet, and I didn't want my gun sitting in it. The walk was about 500 yards through the mud and water. I was drenched from falling in the water and wrestling the ATV for thirty minutes, so I was carrying several extra unwanted pounds.

At the halfway point, I thought I might have been having a heart attack. I couldn't check my symptoms on Google because my iPhone got wet, so I shrugged it off and kept walking.

There was no walking through mud and water. It was more like trudging. That's a better word. And after thirty minutes of trudging—slipping, sliding, stumbling, and bumbling—I reached the cypress tree.

I leaned up against the trunk for a couple of minutes to catch my breath and look up at the sky for ducks. The smooth bark felt good against my cold, wet skin. I picked a spot about twenty-five yards away and sunk my mojo down into the mud. I walked back toward the tree and started looking for a place to rest my gun.

"Wretched gun strap," I thought again. Of all mornings, it had to pick this one to break. After much trial and error, I found a gap in the tree bark that my gun fit perfectly into. "Whew! That's a relief," I thought. At least I wouldn't have to hold my shotgun the entire time I was standing here.

My focus then turned to hunting. I snuggled up next to the tree as my eyes gazed upward toward the dimly lit sky. I could see groups of ducks flying in the distance, but nothing was close enough for me to waste my breath calling at.

After a few more minutes, I noticed a group of mallards flying directly overhead. They just appeared like you would imagine a ghost appearing in your dark bedroom around midnight. Their wingbeats were in perfect rhythm as they soared just below the dark grey clouds. I took cover behind the giant cypress tree and reached for my favorite Echo duck call. I made a few clucks, and the birds turned. One of the drakes liked what I said so much that he came to see me.

He cupped his wings at once and started to drop altitude. I slowly reached for my gun to prepare for the imminent shot. I watched as the mallard drake beautifully soared, cutting through the misty haze and approaching my mojo decoy like he was born for it. This was the kind of sight duck hunters dreamed about. It was an actual thing of beauty watching a mallard drake glide through the air, gracefully falling within shotgun range. As he came about ten feet off the water, he pulled up to fly directly over the decoy. By this time, I had my right hand on the grip of my gun, and in one quick motion, I pulled my Beretta out of the tree, shouldered it, gazed down the barrel, and squeezed the trigger. BOOM! The mallard drake fell from the sky and landed in the water.

In a way, I felt a bit of sadness that the picture-perfect moment was over. There was also a moment of sorrow for ending an animal's life. I grew up hunting, and to this day, I still feel something after taking a game bird or game animal's life. But soon, that sadness turns to joy because I am overwhelmed with thanks for the reward and can look forward to a delicious meal. There is a certain amount of pride that comes with knowing where your food comes from and putting in the work it takes to harvest, clean, and cook it.

I put my gun back on safety and took a couple of steps toward the mallard drake. Soon I noticed the duck had its head up and was looking at me.

This is not an uncommon occurrence while waterfowl hunting. Sometimes a duck is not fatally wounded but instead crippled with a broken wing or knocked out from the impact.

When the duck saw me, he started to swim away. I quickly shouldered my shotgun, placed the bead slightly under his head, and squeezed the trigger. The gun fired, and BBs peppered the water all around the drake, but he kept swimming. So, I raised my shotgun and fired again, BBs peppered all around him once more, but the bird kept swimming. I thought, "How could this be?" I felt my first shot was nearly perfect, and the last two finishing shots struck precisely where they needed to. How was the duck still swimming away? I had to reload my gun after the third shot, and by the time I shouldered it and gazed down the barrel, the bird had swum quite far. I aimed and squeezed off one more desperate round, trying to stop him but still no luck.

At this point, I was just wasting shotgun shells. The duck had swum at least one hundred yards from me, and there was no way my twelve-gauge three-inch magnums could reach him. My picture-perfect moment was ruined by a nonfatal shot. The bird swam down the slough and back in the direction of the busted Honda. I decided we would just have to try and retrieve the duck on our way to getting all my other gear. I could already hear how much crap I was going to catch over my unlucky morning. I slowly walked back to the giant old cypress in defeat with my tail tucked between my legs.

I kept an eye on the swimming duck to make sure he didn't escape the canal. There was nowhere for him to go and nothing for him to hide in, so I was confident we would find him.

I continued to hunt for another thirty minutes before I started to get cold. The temperature was forty-eight degrees, but because I had fallen in the water, the mild forty-eight felt like zero degrees. I stood there and shivered for about fifteen minutes before I decided to move around to warm up.

The other two groups hadn't shot for a while, so I figured the hunt was basically done. I decided that I would abandon my post at the giant dead cypress tree and walk to the group that was about 500 yards down the canal.

For one, I needed to warm up, and the long trudge through the mud and water would certainly do that. Also, I knew if I walked down to the group, I would guarantee they would not leave me stranded on the farm. And since my luck was gone, I figured it was best not to take any chances. So, I began my long, cumbersome walk, shotgun in one hand and mojo decoy in the other.

The guys saw me coming when I was about 200 yards away. They began to gather decoys and collect their gear. As I got close, I started to chuckle about my terrible morning. I could not think of a worse outing in my entire life. Don't get me wrong, stuff happens all the time while out duck hunting: ATV gets stuck, somebody forgets their shells, somebody slips and falls in the water, or somebody misses an easy shot. I have seen these pitfalls over the years. But honestly, I have never seen anything top my morning on December 28th. Between flooding out the Rancher, my iPhone, and the broken mojo, this hunt alone would cost me dearly. And I couldn't put a value on all the pictures and videos I had lost.

Little did I know, this morning was about to get worse, very much worse.

As I approached Micah and David, they both gave me a quick head-to-toe look, and with a grin on Micah's face, he asked, "What the hell happened to you?" I kind of smirked and began to tell them about the past two hours. By the time I finished my story, they were both laughing hysterically. We stood around and awkwardly looked at each other for a moment before Micah asked us what we should do now. We decided to call my cousin David Joe to decide on our next move.

I just wanted to go back to the camp, take off all my wet clothes, and warm up, but I was willing to go along with whatever the group decided. After all, it wasn't their fault I was soaking wet and cold. Micah called David Joe and told him to come pick us up. Shortly after they hung up, I spotted a group of teal flying down the canal toward us. Instinct took over as I knelt, grabbed a shell from my pocket, loaded it in my gun, and watched in anticipation as the teal flew by. But my bad luck trend would continue, and the birds did not pass within range.

Minutes later, David Joe pulled up on the Ranger with his dog, Tito. Tito was a black Labrador retriever and an excellent duck dog, and I had seen him make fantastic retrieves while hunting alongside him. When David Joe saw me standing there, of course, he had to know what happened too. I gave him the skinny and told him I flipped his Rancher off the culvert. He kind of laughed and said, "Well, you have to pay to fix it." I grinned back at him and agreed. I then walked over to the Ranger and laid my gun down in the back. I felt instant relief that I didn't have to carry it in my hands anymore and that this morning's crazy hunt was over. There would be another day, I figured.

But we weren't finished yet. Earlier in the morning, David had knocked down a teal that fell in the field beside us. Since Tito was with us, we put him to work. David Joe sent him on a blind retrieve in the direction pointed out by David. After a couple of minutes, Tito came running back with the teal in his mouth. I wasn't surprised he found the bird; like I said, he was an excellent retriever. I then told David Joe about the bird I had knocked down earlier, and I could still faintly see the last place I saw it. So, David Joe sent Tito after my duck.

The bird was a very long way off for a retrieve. Tito would run about one hundred yards straight back and then run in circles back toward us, trying to pick up the bird's scent. Each time Tito stopped, David Joe would blow the whistle and motion him to keep running. Tito would run another one hundred yards and do the same thing. David Joe blew the whistle at him three more times before he decided the bird was too far.

I told him it was no big deal. We could just ride down in the Ranger and get the duck. He blew the whistle signaling Tito to run back to us. Meanwhile, everybody started to pick up the muddy gear and load it into the bed of the Ranger, and I felt like I had been beaten with a stick.

In a way, I was humbled by my extremely lousy luck that day. It's incredible how we plan something to be so grand in our heads, and due to strange occurrences, our day can turn on us in an instant. I honestly thought that I would have a good hunt that morning. We had scouted the day before, and I knew I had the perfect plan to execute. I was not mad anymore about my misfortunes but instead grateful that I would at least have a funny story to tell.

CHAPTER 3
The Fall

I grabbed my mojo decoy out of the mud and started to slowly make my way around to the passenger side of the Ranger. By this time, my feet were as big as a car rim because of the mud stuck to my boots. One positive thing about the morning was at least I got a good workout in!

Tommy Moffitt's voice popped into my head, "Nobody's gonna die out here today," his famous saying when the team faced a particularly tough summer workout. Boy was I about to put those words to the test.

Working out or exercising had never been my thing, most likely because I was forced to all those years while playing football. I dreaded it in a way only a former college or professional athlete can understand.

I was standing around on the passenger side of the Ranger when Tito came running back up. He was obviously tired, with his tongue flapping about all over his face. I couldn't blame him; I knew he didn't like running in that mud any more than I did. I placed my mojo decoy in a slot on the side of the bed of the Ranger. Tito ran up to the driver's side of the Ranger, and David Joe bent down to help him jump in the back. Tito landed heavily in the Ranger bed; he was exhausted from the long retrieval try for my wounded duck.

And then it happened, something we never dreamed of. One split second changed my life. What would follow would forever burn into the minds of the group.

I was on the passenger side, Micah was standing near the tailgate latch, DJ was on the driver's side, and David was standing a few feet behind Micah. Suddenly a loud crack rang out. We all either didn't realize or couldn't believe what had just happened.

Tito caused the gun to fire.

Somebody screamed out, "What was that?"

I quickly glanced down and noticed a coke can size hole in the Ranger bed sidewall. It quickly dawned on all of us what had just happened, although we didn't want to believe it. A gun just went off!

Their wide concerned eyes looked at me when they noticed the hole beside me. A tingling feeling started to go down my leg. It was then I realized I had been hit. Amazingly, I did not feel any pain as the BBs tore through my flesh. My first thought was maybe it wasn't that bad. I took a step back to make sure, but when I did, my left leg did not move. I lost my balance and started to fall back toward the muddy ground. That's when the adrenaline rush coursed through my body. I screamed out in fear! "Was this a dream?" I thought to myself. "Did this actually just happen? It's time to wake up! Wake up, Matt!"

I quickly knew that this was serious. I never saw my leg after it had been shot. How I knew the shot could be fatal was by the way my body reacted. Everything suddenly started to close in around me, and my panic turned into a calmer state. I felt like I could drift off to sleep any second. It was like somebody had sucked all the energy out of my body, and I was paralyzed. This was worse than a nightmare. Seconds earlier, I was up walking around laughing and chatting with my friends, and the next, I was lying in the mud gasping for air.

Micah and David ran over to where I was lying. Micah yelled at David Joe to call 911. Micah and David picked me up and tried to load me into the bed of the Ranger. Before they dropped me in, David Joe screamed at them to load me in the front seat. I don't know why he did this, but this allowed me to sit up and apply pressure to my leg.

Things quickly worsened. Right as they slid me into the front seat, my vision went black. I was completely blind. I could not see anything. Amazingly, I didn't panic. My vision was the least of my concerns as I sat up in the front seat and started to experience what I perceived as the act of dying.

Because I had on chest waders, the guys did not know how badly I was bleeding, but I did. My blood was contained in my waders, and only a little was visible on my hands and leg. Micah jumped in the back of the Ranger as David Joe hopped in the driver's seat. Tito was also in the bed of the Ranger with Micah. David stayed behind to tell my younger brother, Connor, who was still hunting, what had happened.

As David Joe drove through the field, he and Micah discussed where they should take me. They could take me back to the camp or drive me to the highway, which would be closer for the ambulance. Since it was about the same distance to both places, they decided to take me to the highway. David Joe handed Micah the phone to continue talking to the 911 operator.

As David Joe drove, I remember thinking to myself, "If we get stuck out here, I'm a dead man." I may have said a quick prayer to not get stuck; I can't really remember.

David Joe was driving like a madman through the mud. I was still blind, but his fast driving and hard turns were jerking my body all around and kept me from passing out. All I could do at this point was stay awake and pray.

Strangely, my vision started to come back. I remember looking at David Joe's face, and his eyes were big as saucers as he glanced at me to make sure I was still with him.

I knew I was dying; I had never felt this way before, and I had pushed my body to extreme limits in my short life. The best way I can describe my dying experience was being constantly on the verge of falling asleep. It was a dreamlike state, colors were brighter, and time felt slower. I was struggling to breathe while holding a completely numb and tingling left leg.

As we neared the highway, I started to gaze out over the farm. There was a light haze dancing over the top of the fertile silty clay loam soil while naked winter-beaten trees loomed overhead. It is amazing the details I can remember from that day. An eerie stillness hung in the air while I tried to keep myself from a gruesome panic overtaking my thoughts.

Instead, I came to grips with the fact that this may be the last sight of this giant blue planet I called home I would ever see.

I sensed an evil presence lurking as I was hit with thoughts of regrets and wrongdoings in my life. I feared where these thoughts would lead if I allowed myself to drift off to sleep for the last time. I began to panic and fought with the remaining strength I had left to not allow these painful memories to lull me into unending darkness. All I could think to do was recite what I had seen in the movies when somebody was lying there dying. Everybody was screaming, “Stay with me, stay awake!” Staying awake was my only goal in life at that moment.

When we got to the highway, I was in bad shape. It was becoming more and more difficult to breathe, and I was in total dismay. As we parked alongside the highway, Micah and David Joe grabbed me and laid me on the embankment. There was a steep drop-off on the side of the road, so they laid my head on the downslope, leaving my leg well above my head.

Due to all the commotion, Tito jumped out of the Ranger onto the ground. David Joe had put a short leash on him so he wouldn’t run off. The leash was too short, and he had hung himself halfway. I saw this and told them to save Tito and not worry about me.

I was gasping for air at this point and started to lose it. Death had come for me, and there was nothing I could do to stop it. My labored breathing turned into a panic attack, and I kept screaming, “I’m going to die! I can’t breathe!” I felt as if I was falling back into myself, and the world was collapsing in on me. I didn’t dare turn around and look down. I felt an endless black pit that would swallow me whole as soon as I let go and closed my eyes. I fought with every bit of strength I had left to stay on this earth if possible.

My friends tried to comfort me and started telling me how tough I was, and how I wouldn’t let a few BBs kill me. They kept saying that the gunshot didn't look bad, and the ambulance was close. I knew they were wrong. There was no way a human body could feel the way mine did without being on the verge of death.

As I lay on the side of the road bleeding out, my mind started to drift. I began to think about my one-year-old son Barrett. I felt an overwhelming sadness that my beautiful little boy would have to go through life without his daddy. Not only would I not be there for him going forward, but he would have no memory of me at all.

I tried to imagine if I would have had to go through my life with questions and not having my dad there for guidance. I wondered how the repercussions of the way I was killed would negatively affect my son's life. How would this story be told to him one day? Would he feel sorry for me, for himself? The fear for my little boy overshadowed all the physical pain I felt from a point-blank twelve-gauge shotgun blast. If you are a parent, I'm sure you understand. I tried to think back to our last moments together; I couldn't even remember if I kissed and hugged him goodbye days earlier.

My thoughts then wandered to my wife, Liana. I was terrified for her. She would have to deal with this overwhelming tragedy that could possibly haunt and affect her for the remainder of her life, all while raising our precious son alone. I hoped if she found somebody else one day, he would treat our son like his own, and maybe this would help make up for my tragic death. These heavy thoughts continued to bounce around in my head for the remainder of my consciousness.

The first responders to arrive on the scene were a couple of volunteer firefighters who lived in Eagle Lake, Mississippi.

My physical world was becoming foggy, while my spiritual world was more alive than ever. I was in a dream-like state, getting a 10,000-foot view of my life.

A slow death is a clear moment of self-reflection. There are no excuses, or "I'll do better next time." You are faced with the truth of your life and what you desire above all else.

In that moment, my heart's deepest desires, money, and power brought me no peace, comfort, or love. Instead, I got a glimpse of the hell my life had slowly become.

One of the firemen came to my side and cut my waders off. When he peeled my waders back, I heard someone say, "Oh my God." Blood poured from my waders like water from a pitcher, and my clothes were stained red. This didn't surprise me.

When you are dying, you are fully aware of it. You're not guessing that you might die or could die. You know you are dying.

The next fireman ran up, and they both placed a tourniquet above my wound. It had been at least twenty minutes since I had been shot, and I lost a lot of blood. In fact, I was on the verge of bleeding out at that point. After days of surgeries, the doctors told my family that my femoral artery was directly hit and that the artery itself looked like hamburger meat.

The other fireman ran back over to me with an oxygen mask. They placed it over my nose and mouth and cranked it up. I started screaming at them, "I can't breathe," and fear came over me. I pulled the mask off and yelled louder, "I can't breathe," so they turned the oxygen up all the way and placed the mask back on my face. I screamed at them again, "I can't breathe," and I started to rip the mask off once more.

Everybody started telling me to calm down, and the ambulance was almost there. This helped me calm down a little, but really, I believe I was beginning to accept my fate. I had my mind made up that I would die, and there was nothing I or anyone else could do about it. I started to fall in and out of consciousness right before the ambulance arrived.

They loaded me on the stretcher and into the back of the ambulance. I felt weightless as gravity gently rocked my body through the winding curves in the road. I looked up and noticed a blinding light above me where I could make out the faceless figure looming over me. It was that of the paramedic looking down over me just before the darkness finally came.

I got myself into this situation, and I did not have the ability to get myself out. I was powerless as to whether I would ever see the light again.

CHAPTER 4
Back Home

Liana

I was home meal prepping for Barrett and cleaning up the house after a big family Christmas just three days before. As Matt's wife, I never even gave the duck hunt or what was going on there a second thought. It was just part of our lives. We had dinner plans with our friends Laura and Will that night, so he had better make it home.

Matt and I had built this cookie-cutter starter home four years earlier. It was our first home and was the perfect size for the two of us. Now that there were three of us, things were getting a little tight. Gone were the days of a fresh candle and a glass of wine at dinner. The house now smelled of baby food and poop diapers while an endless pot of coffee was brewed to help us power through the sleepless nights. Even though there were fond memories within these walls, Matt and I considered getting a bigger home soon.

I glanced at my iPhone and noticed I had two missed calls from David Joe and two missed calls from Matt's brother Jake. This seemed rather strange. I thought maybe Matt's phone had died, and he was using David Joe's, but I couldn't think of a reason why Jake had also called me.

I called David Joe back, expecting Matt to answer. David Joe picked up, and I could barely understand what he said. The phone was cutting in and out, and after several attempts, I understood what he was trying to say. Matt had been shot.

My stomach sank as these life-changing words sunk in. As a hunter's wife, I always had fears and thoughts that something could go wrong. These seemingly silly fears became my new reality, and I had no time to process them. Jake then started beeping in over the phone while somebody abruptly banged on the door simultaneously.

"What is happening?" I thought to myself.

I opened the heavy wooden front door to find my sister-in-law, Haley. I was relieved to see a familiar face who may have more information. She reached out to hug me in the doorway and tried to put me at ease with her usual chipper and positive tone. Haley is a nurse, so she manages these types of situations regularly.

Thankfully, Haley and Jake had already created a plan. I was trapped in my own terrifying thoughts as she began to tell me the next steps. She was there to keep Barrett, and I needed to pack a bag. Jake was coming to pick me up, and we were going to Vicksburg, where Matt was heading to the hospital. I gave Haley quick instructions about feeding Barrett and started packing.

I walked in circles around our bedroom, not knowing what I should grab. Worrying about what I wore or looked like was the last thing on my mind. I put on some comfy workout clothes, and a pair of black UGG boots, and threw my hair up in a clippie. I had no idea how long I would be gone. I was thinking no more than a night or two. I saw a scared little girl looking back at me as I gazed into the bathroom mirror. I took a deep breath, closed my eyes, and told myself everything would be okay.

I hugged and kissed Barrett goodbye, not knowing the terrible world I was about to enter. I had never stayed away from Barrett a night in his life. I barely left him his whole first year. Our families can tell you that I rarely ask for help and spend every minute with him. I love him so much, and I truly enjoyed every second of being a mom. He is my world.

Jake picked me up at 10:30 a.m. and seemed calm, so I stayed calm. I climbed up in his brown Chevrolet truck and buckled my seat belt. Simply being told my husband was shot left my mind open to race and imagining horrible scenarios. I asked Jake all he knew about the situation. He knew Matt had been shot in the leg, but he didn't think it was severe. He kept describing the scene from Wedding Crashers when Vince Vaughn humorously gets peppered in the butt as an example. I began to imagine greeting Matt in the emergency room, half-mad at him for scaring me and half-smiling that he was okay.

I called my mom and told her Matt had been shot, and it wasn't anything significant. I asked her if she could go to my house after work to keep Barrett, and I thought I would be back that night with Matt. I was still clueless about the nightmare that was beginning to unfold.

As Jake drove, we engaged in small talk. I asked him about Haley and what their life plans were. Neither of us wanted to discuss the elephant in the truck. As we got closer to Vicksburg, I started to sense things weren't quite like they seemed. Haley called Jake, and the call went through his truck speaker. The tone in her voice didn't sound like this was no big deal. There was a new nervousness that masked her usual chipper tone. We then got a call from Matt's Aunt Evelyn. She told us he was currently in surgery.

My mind started to spiral out of control, and it would continue to spiral to depths that I didn't know were possible. Hearing these words hurt and scared me. I distinctly remember looking up at the ceiling of the truck, holding my face, and saying, "Oh my God," trying not to start crying. I began to panic as Jake told me it would be okay. I wanted to believe him, but that was becoming difficult.

As we crossed the Mississippi River bridge, I gazed out over the fog-covered murky water, wondering if I would ever see my husband's smile again.

When Jake and I arrived at the hospital, David, Dan, and Evelyn were already there. As we approached the group, I tried to read the expressions on their faces. No one looked upset, so I believed this to be a good sign. Evelyn came over to me, hugged me, and disclosed more details about Matt's condition. She told me he was in surgery, and they were doing everything possible to save his life. Then she uttered two words that nearly made my heart stop: femoral artery. I had taken a couple of anatomy classes in college, and I knew how vital the femoral artery was.

In short minutes, I went from my husband being braised by a bullet to my husband in surgery, fighting for his life. I feared I might pass out. I felt so anxious and scared that I couldn't fully process what was happening. Was this reality or a dream? I felt as if the dial on the gravity was turned to max power as I seemingly melted to the floor. I stepped away to call my mom to tell her what I had been told. My mom is a nurse, so "she can explain the situation," I thought.

Mom did not believe me when I told her his femoral artery was hit. She said, "Surely not, Liana. We don't need to think be thinking like that." She, like me, tries to be positive and not overreact. We ended the conversation about how she would watch Barrett until I returned home, hopefully, that night. I then walked back into the cold, bleakly decorated waiting room and sat down in the uncomfortable rigid metal chair as The Weather Channel played loudly on the TV.

Matt's large family began to fill the waiting room to max capacity with over fifty people. Some tried to walk around and stay busy while others sat silently and looked at the tile floor. Others tried to make small talk with me, but I was not interested. When I got the courage to look up, everyone around me kept giving me long, blank stares.

The looks from the guys Matt was hunting with that day were especially troubling. They had seen with their eyes why everybody was gathering in the hospital waiting room. They didn't have to say anything, their facial expressions spoke loud enough.

It was hard to fully grasp what was happening. Did everybody else seem to know something I didn't? Why was everybody whispering and in such a somber mood? I tried to ignore their strange behavior, but this was impossible for me. So, I looked down at the tile floor and kept to myself.

I've always processed my internal thoughts. I didn't need constant conversation for reassurance. Internally, I'm rational, so I reasoned that everything would be okay. Calm as a cucumber or Positive Polly are some of the nicknames I've earned through my years as an elementary school teacher.

I stuck to my usual defense mechanism of suppressing my emotions. Before allowing myself to panic, I first needed to talk to the doctor. I rationalized I was not about to lose my husband and be widowed at twenty-eight while being made a single mother with a one-year-old son.

The chiming of my phone seemed endless as texts started coming in when the news got around. How was I supposed to respond when I didn't know what was going on or what exactly happened? I didn't know how the gun had gone off, how the dog was involved, nothing. No one sat me down and explained what had happened. They were most likely scared of how I would react to the unbelievable details.

I would overhear whispers, and I picked up on bits and pieces. It wasn't that I didn't want to know. At the time, I feared knowing would make things worse. Sitting quietly to myself felt like the best option.

When I heard it was Matt's gun that went off, I couldn't believe it. In fact, I didn't believe it. Matt had always been so careful with guns. Matt was a cautious person in general. He was never reckless and had always been adamant about gun safety anytime I went hunting with him.

Hours passed before people moved downstairs to the cafeteria to eat. There was no way I would stomach anything, but I went along with everybody so I wouldn't have to wait alone. After sitting down at the cafeteria-style table, someone handed me a red biohazard bag of Matt's belongings.

Without hesitating to think why the items were in a biohazard bag, I reached in for the wallet I had bought Matt. When I grasped it, I had to fight off an urge to throw up as I noticed the contents were covered in cold, wet blood, Matt's cold, wet blood. I couldn't breathe, my heart pounded, and I ripped my hand out of the bag like I had found a rattlesnake in the bottom. Did somebody just casually hand me a bag of Matt's blood-soaked belongings? I quickly looked up to see if anyone noticed and wiped the blood off my hand on my lululemon yoga pants.

Touching the cold, wet blood woke me up, and I then fully understood that this was not a dream. This was real, and my husband was in serious trouble.

Every so often, a call from the operating room would come in. We would get a status update on the timeframe Matt would remain in surgery. Because David was the first to arrive, he was the initial contact. Each time his phone rang, my heart dropped, and I held my breath. They asked to change the OR's contact to me to take the calls. This made me uneasy, so I declined. I didn't know if I wanted to be the one to give everybody the unsettling news. A phone call was all I had to know if Matt was still alive.

After what felt like an eternity, Dr. Ferris and a nurse came to the waiting room. I jumped up out of my chair when I saw them coming. I thought, "Okay, finally, some news. I'll finally be told everything is okay. Matt is going to be fine." However, that was not the feeling I got from seeing the doctor's face.

As I stood at arm's length with our family huddled behind me, I saw defeat and sadness in Dr. Ferris's eyes. I glanced at his nurse and saw tears running down her cheeks. I thought they were about to tell me Matt was dead, and I would never see my husband alive again.

When Dr. Ferris opened his mouth to speak, he hesitated while choking on tears. He told us they had done everything they could at this point. Matt needed to be moved to a more advanced trauma unit. I can't imagine how you would feel with so many hopeful faces staring at you, clinging to every word you say.

They didn't offer us any hope. They had none to give. All they could tell us was Matt needed to be airlifted to Jackson, Mississippi. There wasn't any explanation for what happened in the operating room.

I hugged them both and thanked them for trying to save my husband. Matt's family wanted more answers, but no answers were given. Matt's life was in God's hands now. Everyone began to cry and hug each other, trying to find solace. The mood in the room quickly transitioned to somber and quiet a little after 3 p.m. I signed a consent form for Matt to be airlifted to Jackson.

I rode with Matt's dad Mark and stepmom, Amy, to Jackson. No one uttered a word. Mark gently rested his hand on my back while driving us I-20 eastbound to Jackson. I can't imagine where his thoughts were at that moment.

I started to replay every detail about Matt and my life together. Good, bad, funny, and embarrassing memories flashed through my mind like they were playing on an old movie reel. I prayed to God that we had more memories to make, but my faith faded more by the second. All I knew was Matt's life was in jeopardy, and they were also trying to save his leg. It was too much to bear, but somehow, I did it.

CHAPTER 5
Consuming Chaos

Walking into the UMMC ER was shocking. This is a vast hospital, the largest in Mississippi. And people were running around in a seemingly organized chaos talking with patients. We approached the check-in desk and were told Matt had not arrived yet. "How did we beat the helicopter?" I thought. I started feeling the worst had happened. Had he died? Did he even make it in the helicopter?

The UMMC emergency room was a terrible place to deal with the type of crisis I faced. People all around us were obviously in pain and dealing with their own specific tragedies, which did not seem to compare to mine. We sat and waited to get word on Matt's arrival.

Nobody in the ER knew anything about his status. The whole day we were left in the dark and spoon-fed vague information. This couldn't possibly be where I was supposed to await news of my dying husband. Finally, a staff member escorted us to a small, private waiting room. Still, no one had any new information on Matt's arrival.

A while later, we were escorted to the SICU waiting room. This is where our request for more information was granted. I soon understood why everybody had been reluctant to share the details.

Mark sat slumped on the floor with his back against a corner of a wall. He was white as a sheet and looked confused and unsure if this was our reality.

"Are you okay?" I asked.

He replied, "I guess," while staring blankly at the floor.

David walked up, hugged me, and said, "You're a hell of a lot stronger than I am." He was surprised and couldn't believe I felt the need to check on someone else. Little did I know how strong I would have to be. So far, this day had been a walk in the park compared to what was just around the corner.

David then began sharing what he had been told by the paramedics who had transported Matt to the hospital in Vicksburg. When he said the word coded, I took a step back.

"Wait, what do you mean 'coded'?" I asked.

"Yeah, he coded for the first time in the ambulance. They were able to revive him. Then he coded again at the hospital. They said he was angry and trying to yank the tube out of his throat," David explained.

Mark's face turned a shade whiter as he looked at me in complete disbelief. Neither of us had any idea Matt had already coded and had been revived.

"What?" I asked. "How did I not know any of this?"

Matt's dad said, "I don't even think I really know what's going on." Shaking his head in disbelief

Confusion and chaos continued circulating around the room.

By this time, over one hundred people had shown up for support, and we had to move back out to the hospital lobby. We waited for a long time before receiving any news. A resident doctor would let us know Matt was still in surgery about every hour. We were given a glimmer of hope when one update revealed he had given the nurse a thumbs up.

As night began to fall, Dr. Baldwin came out to give us in-depth details of the situation. Same as Vicksburg, I jumped up and ran toward him, nearly tripping in the process. He waved his hands at me and told me I should probably sit down. My heart sank, and I walked back to my chair. He explained that Matt could die at any second. He told me they couldn't stop the blood loss, and the only way to control it was to amputate his left leg to the knee. He clearly said this was a matter of life or death.

It felt like someone sucker-punched me in the stomach. How was this possible? How did this day continue to get worse?

Dr. Baldwin needed my consent to move forward with the amputation. I had to hastily make this decision with an audience of over one hundred people. The eyes of our entire family, along with friends, were staring at me. I didn't want to make such a life-altering decision like this. I wanted to talk to Matt, but that wasn't possible. The doctor reassured me that my husband would die if I didn't grant permission for the amputation. All I could think was how devastated Matt would be.

I somehow found the strength to process the decision. I looked toward Matt's dad for reassurance, and he nodded and put his head down. I took the doctor's pen and signed off on the amputation. Dr. Baldwin and his team hurried back to the OR to begin the surgery. With the quick stroke of a pen, my life would be forever changed. This decision could not be undone. I prayed Matt would understand and forgive me.

The weight of so many eyes staring at me was suffocating, to say the least. I wanted to scream out in anger to God and ask why this was happening. People were all around watching as my life fell apart like it was right off the script of a dramatic blockbuster movie. All I kept thinking of was how devastated Matt would be. He was very independent and didn't like asking for help from anybody. He had the "We will do whatever you want if we do it my way" type of personality.

In an argument we had one night about me not doing a simple task the way he wanted it done, I snapped back at him. "It would drive you crazy to lose control of everything being done your way." Little did I know that this exact scenario would play out later in our lives.

This surgery was not supposed to take over an hour to complete. After the one-hour mark, everyone started to fear the worst had happened. Dr. Miguel would periodically come out and give brief updates. He would show up teary-eyed with worry and stress all over his face each time.

Finally, after two hours, he appeared and explained that they had somewhat stabilized Matt to remove him from the operating room. He stressed how very, very sick he was, and his life balanced on a razor's edge. Matt was being kept alive with machines and the grace of God at this point.

Matt's grandmother spoke up from behind me and asked, "But can you tell us for certain if he is going to live?"

Dr. Miguel's' response was simple: "Ma'am, I can't. All I can say is he's fighting for his life." The doctor wanted to give us hope, but there was none to be had that day.

They wouldn't tell us for sure if they believed Matt would make it through the night. He made it clear they would do all they could, but his chance of survival was meager. I hugged Dr. Miguel and thanked him for trying to save my husband. They had bought my husband a little more time on this earth, and I was thankful for that.

At that point, my emotions started to derail. I couldn't breathe. I couldn't think straight. I couldn't even cry. I felt utterly empty and heartbroken. I grew numb inside and felt a dead weight in the center of my chest.

I needed space. I had to get away from all the hushed comments and sad stares. I stood up and hurriedly walked toward the door. I had no idea where I was going, but I needed to move to feel something. Someone got up to follow me, so I quickly scurried away. As I burst through the door, I heard my Meme say, "Give her space."

I walked and walked down halls that all looked the same. I had no sense of direction and didn't know where I was or how I would get through this day. When I thought about our son Barrett, I began to sob uncontrollably. After crying for a moment and pulling my hands from my face, I realized I HAD TO GO BACK. I had to be strong to make decisions that would affect our little boy. It had been over twelve hours since I left Barrett. Right then, it hit me how devastating this could be to his life.

FLASHBACK

February 2017

I didn't think Matt would ever be ready to have a baby. All my life, I dreamed of having children of my own. My childhood nickname was Nanny. I always had the instinct to take care of others. If I saw a way to help, I wanted to do my part.

My mom was a single parent for much of my childhood, so I really got to fill the shoes of the caretaker role with my three sisters. When I was six, after my mom remarried, her husband adopted my sisters and me. When we found out we were getting another little sister, I was thrilled! It was a big year in my young life.

Not long after my parents announced the upcoming arrival of my youngest sister, my dad suddenly and tragically passed away. He went for a jog, came home to rest, and suffered from a heart event. This left my mom raising three girls again on her own while pregnant with a fourth girl.

I tried my best to help pick up the pieces by assisting my mom in whatever way I could. Nanny wasn't just a nickname anymore; it was a role I took to heart. I loved my sisters, and I loved helping my mom through that difficult period in our lives.

Every time I brought up having a baby, Matt's response was, "We aren't financially ready yet." Or he needed more time to work his way up through his company.

I never understood his viewpoint of putting life on hold for money. I've always focused on relationships and living life over financial success. Matt was the total opposite. Even in high school, when most teenagers barely had two nickels to rub together, Matt had his own cash saved up. I never saw him ask his parents for money; never a spender, always a saver.

One ordinary morning out of the blue, I was in utter disbelief when he woke up, turned to me, and said, "Let's have a baby!" My heart nearly leaped from my chest!

"Really? Are you being serious?" I asked.

Matt would often tease me about this very thing, so I wasn't buying it at first. When he told me he was serious, I couldn't believe it. None of our friends had started trying to have kids yet. This would make us the first. When I asked him why he had a sudden change of heart, he couldn't explain himself. He said he just had a feeling when he woke up that morning. I was scared to ask too many more questions for fear of him changing his mind.

On February 8, I took a pregnancy test. This also happens to be Matt and my anniversary. That evening, Matt cooked us up steaks, baked potatoes, and a salad, his specialty. He has always been the better chef.

While he was distracted with making dinner, I snuck back into our master bathroom and took a pregnancy test. I had already decided that I wouldn't say anything if it was negative because it may ruin our anniversary dinner. When the smiley face appeared, my jaw dropped.

I was pregnant! I had been dreaming of this moment for years, and here it was! I did my best at hiding my smile when I walked out to the living room to tell Matt the news. I proudly walked up, handed him my glass of wine, and said, "Here, I won't be needing this anymore."

His first response was, "Why?"

The biggest grin spread across my face, and I said, "You know why!"

His face turned ghost white and sagged from the weight of my news. "Are you sure that the test is correct?"

He asked at least thirty times that night. He spent the rest of the evening in a daze of questions about insurance and childcare costs. I was a little frustrated with his lack of romance, but I knew he would come around after he got all the financial stuff sorted out in his head.

When the doctor confirmed the test was right, I could not hold my excitement! My dream was now my reality! Two months later, we found out our baby would be a boy. I had prayed every night that my first child would be a boy and that he would look just like his daddy!

Barrett Miles Branch joined our family on October 5, 2017. He was beautiful, with strawberry blonde hair and the cutest tiny lips. This time in our lives with our newborn son was extraordinary. I was absolutely smitten with Barrett and wanted to spend every second of my day snuggling and loving on him. We were so proud of our son. Life seemed to be moving in the exact direction I wanted. I felt I was finally being who I was always meant to be, a mom. I truly loved every second of it and had a tough time returning to work after maternity leave.

Barrett's first birthday came and went in the blink of an eye. Our baby was no longer counted in months but in years. That was hard for me to grasp. Time just seems to fly by ten times faster when you have a child.

Right when we felt like we had this whole parenting thing kind of figured out and had plans to try for a second child that winter, our world was flipped upside down. In one phone call, the course of Barrett and my life was changed forever.

CHAPTER 6
Real-Life Horror

The hospital staff warned me before being allowed to see Matt that night. They explained that he would not be recognizable and was severely swollen, Michelin Man swollen. They also explained he was in a coma and not responsive.

I waited anxiously outside the metal double doors of the SICU. They were kept locked to keep people from entering. Only immediate family was allowed to enter. I took slow, heavy breaths just before the staff buzzed us in. Since I had never been inside an intensive care unit before, I did not know what to expect. The only sounds I heard were the beeping machines and the soft patter of my slow footsteps. I followed a nurse who escorted me past rooms with glass entrance walls. My eyes wandered as I tried to take in my strange surroundings. Patients filled every room, and most were lying unresponsive.

As we walked farther down the hall, each patient I passed looked worse than the one before. It smelled like a mixture of formaldehyde, body fluids, and disinfectant marinating in musty air. It was difficult to take in without becoming nauseated.

I considered sprinting past the nurse to get to Matt's room faster, but I held off on this urge. Instead, I cautiously stayed behind the nurse as we slowly made our way down the dimly lit hall. I didn't know if I could handle seeing my husband like this. "Is this the last time I will ever see him?" I thought.

When I got to his door, I took a deep breath, said a quick prayer, and braced myself for the horror of which I had been warned. As I stepped into his cramped room, I froze. The space was full of doctors and nurses working frantically. I glanced toward the bed, and tears fell from my eyes.

"This is not my husband," I thought. It looked as if death had already taken him. He was swollen to three times his normal size. The bright fluorescent lights highlighted his dead gray, lifeless skin that perfectly matched the color of the fog skating over the Mississippi River. The only thing that kept him alive was the machines he was attached to by numerous wires and tubes. I had never seen anything like this in the movies.

I rested my hands on his puffy hand and watched as the machines violently pumped his chest up and down. The hardest thing to look at was his slightly cracked open eyes that never blinked. I looked deep into them for a sign of my husband, but there was no life there. I pleaded with him that this couldn't be the ending to our story. This wouldn't be my last memory.

"Barrett needs you. I need you." I cried. "We are supposed to have more children to love on."

I begged him to fight, to stay here with us. I knew he was tired, and I was proud of him for fighting this long, but he had to keep going. I wept, and my heart was completely and utterly broken.

I hopelessly looked toward a doctor in the room and dug deep to find the strength to ask, "Is he even going to make it?" I didn't believe it was possible for anyone who looked like my husband to survive, and I needed the truth.

The doctor responded softly, "Well, there is a slight chance. That's why we are doing all of this."

Then I noticed his missing leg. "Oh, what did I allow them to do to him?" I thought. Even if Matt somehow miraculously woke up, I knew he wouldn't want to live like this.

One of the nurses handed me a bag with his wedding ring in it. I felt my heart ripped from my chest. Time seemed to freeze, I was speechless and numb. I looked at the nurses silently, begging for their help. None of them wanted to make eye contact with me. I noticed one nurse by the IV bag lifted her shoulder to wipe a tear from her cheek. They didn't want me to see they were losing hope.

Medically, his chance of survival was near impossible. His organs had gone septic and were ready to throw in the towel.

Matt's family members standing behind me were silent. The only sound in the room was the constant beeping of machines and my husband's heavy, labored breathing. One by one, Matt's mom, dad, and brother each took turns saying how much they loved him and urged him to keep fighting. Everyone believed this would be the last time they ever saw their son or brother. No one knows exactly what to say in a time like that. Our eyes screamed, "He's gone," while our hearts longed for more time.

Matt's dad gently put his hand on my shoulder to pull me away when it was time to go, but I refused to leave.

I said, "I can't leave him like this! I won't leave! I have to stay!" I could never walk out of that room, knowing Matt's last breath could be at any moment. My husband wouldn't die alone.

Matt's dad looked at the nurses to see if it was okay. One of them silently nodded and whispered it was. If I was forced to leave, there was no way I could keep my sanity after seeing him in that condition.

Matt's nurse did everything she could to keep me going through the night. I'll never forget her. She was friendly and did her best to keep me distracted from my dying husband. We talked about her family, and she asked questions about Matt and my life. I told her happy memories like how we met in high school, dated through college, and got married. I told her about our son Barrett. She would talk to me until I became too tired to speak, then she would leave me so I could sort through my thoughts.

A chair sat very low to the ground for me to sit in. Because I'm so small that I had to sit on my knees to be close enough to hold his hand. I did this until my legs were throbbing and numb. I begged and begged Matt to stay alive all through the first night. I would cry, sit in silence, and pray.

At one point, I tried to rest my head on Matt's hand, hoping the feeling of his touch would soothe me. The contact I felt was not Matt's familiar warm, inviting touch I remembered. This touch was cold, lifeless, full of the unknown, and heartbreak.

I became utterly exhausted and could no longer keep my eyes open. I curled up in the uncomfortable chair and prayed myself to sleep. Maybe Matt would still be alive when I woke up. I dozed off for about two hours. This would be the last bit of sleep I would get for the next two days. How could I sleep and take the chance I would miss getting to tell the love of my life goodbye?

When shift change started at 4:30 a.m., I had to leave the SICU so the nurses could take care of their duties. I could return at 9:00 a.m. I wanted to beg that they make an exception this one time and allow me to stay, but I knew they had already broken too many rules on my behalf. I held Matt's hand and hugged and kissed him as if this would be our last moment on earth together and left the room.

It's hard to explain the feeling when your body experiences shock and grief of this magnitude. My body reacted as if Matt had died when I left that room. My heart refused to beat, and my head and legs felt like concrete center blocks were attached. Each step I took felt monumental.

With my heart shattered into a million pieces, I walked out of the locked metal double doors of the SICU. Deep down, I knew I might never see Matt alive again, but somehow, I managed to step away for a short period.

CHAPTER 7
Survival at Any Cost

To everyone's surprise, Matt survived that first night. He was receiving pressers and blood transfusions around the clock to keep his blood pressure up and help his body cope with the amputation. Alerts on monitors were constantly going off because his oxygen and blood pressure kept falling too low. His life was preserved by constant medical intervention. The vascular surgeons spent the weekend deciding how to let his body heal while rebuilding his obliterated vascular system. Matt living through this was still a giant question mark at this point.

I made sure either I or a family member was always at Matt's side.

The surgeons needed to fix the first problem due to his damaged femoral artery; the blood flowing to his leg had nowhere to go. Matt was constantly bleeding out and needed an endless supply of blood transfusions. The nurses used a marker to write on a glass wall in the room to keep a count of the units of blood Matt had been given. To be transparent, a unit of blood is equal to one pint. The wall was covered in marks in three days.

Matt went in for vascular revision surgery on December 30th. The rebuilding of his vascular system was very complicated. They had to use veins to take the place of a major artery. This was the first revision surgery to help fix the blood flow. The problem then became the constantly dying muscle surrounding his newly built vascular system. This could result in a vascular blowout, which was immediately life-threatening. After surgery consultation, we received news of his body's poor condition, and we were not out of the woods. I wanted them to tell me my husband would be okay, but those words never came.

To help pass the time, I would call Matt's cell phone to hear his voicemail. I didn't know if I would ever hear that familiar voice again. While watching him, I replayed every word he spoke on his voicemail and imagined him waking up and saying those exact words. I longed for his laugh and the twinkle in his eye as he played with Barrett on the living room floor. I tried to stay positive and believe he would come back to me, but I had a hard time convincing myself.

I made fast friends with the staff in the ICU. They graciously allowed me to sleep in Matt's room instead of requiring me to sleep in the ICU family room. The standard policy required that one support person was with the patient during the day, except during shift change.

At night, the support person was supposed to leave the ICU and sleep in the family room outside the unit. This family room was open to the public. People off the street would often visit this dark room looking for a warm place to stay the night. A small woman my size had no business wandering the UMMC campus alone at night. I will be forever thankful to the ICU staff that allowed me to stay with Matt around the clock the entire time he was there.

When I got back to Matt's room on the morning of December 31st, his nurse didn't have a positive update. She explained they still hadn't been able to stop giving him blood, and they were out of options.

"All we can do is wait and see if Matt's body would respond to the vascular changes, she said unenthusiastically."

My heart sank, and I looked at her with tears in my eyes and asked, "Is this it?"

She assured me that I would be notified if we got to that point. I took a breath and thought, "So he isn't going to die today, hopefully."

I then tried to return to a positive mood and continued telling Matt stories about our lives. Looking back, I don't know if I was just telling them to him or to myself to keep my mind occupied with positive thoughts.

Later that morning, Matt's machines started beeping more than usual. The nurse came in and started checking the machines to discover what was causing his vitals to drop. After finding nothing wrong with the machines, she went to Matt's bedside to check his wound. When she pulled back the sheet, we both saw a large amount of blood pooling in the bed. Something was seriously wrong. The blood was not flowing into the wall vac. I quickly stepped back out of her way and watched in horror as two other nurses rushed in. They began working at once and speedily determined Matt needed to go into the OR as soon as possible.

I suddenly realized I was in the way and needed to get out of the room. I stood out of the way in the corner as they wheeled Matt out of the room. All I could think to do was take a mental picture. I wanted desperately to hug and tell him I loved him in case the worst happened. Sadly, I was starting to get used to the possibility that any second could be his last.

Once I cleared the cold metal SICU doors, I called Matt's parents. I frantically explained how he was bleeding out and had to be rushed into emergency surgery. They needed to leave the hotel and come back to the hospital immediately. After getting off the phone with Mark and Amy, I called my mom and lost all control of my emotions alone in the spacious hospital lobby. I sobbed and told her what had happened.

"If they continue with these operations trying to save his leg, my husband is going to die!" I screamed.

This process was very frustrating for the doctors and me. Matt's life and his quality of life were at odds. We all knew his body could only take so many operations before it could go no further. I feared this nightmare would never end.

The lobby was busy and full of people eating lunch, talking, and having a typical day. I would have given anything to go back to my everyday life at that moment. Through my tear-filled blurry vision, I made my way to a column along a wall I could hide behind.

With my back against the column, I slumped down to the floor, pulled my knees to my chest, and let out all the emotions I had been holding in since I had arrived four days earlier. Afraid and all alone, I sat and wept as my life crumbled down all around me.

Mark and Amy found me still crying in the lobby a while later. They sat on the ground, wrapped their arms around me, and tried to soothe me. It was clear I was not in a good place. Amy tried to take what I had said and reassure me that this was good. It was good that Matt was bleeding out and being operated on again. This meant that they would stop the constant blood flow out and improve Matt's health.

After a couple of hours, two surgeons came out to discuss the procedure. They told us the bleeding had been stopped, and Matt was stable. That was it. For a moment, I thought maybe I had overreacted. I had been trying so hard to suppress my emotions since arriving at the hospital. This was the first time I had lost all control. I knew I had to keep fighting to stay strong and be there to make decisions for my husband.

Chaos was my new normal. From one minute to the next, I could be signing surgery consent forms and then busily arranging childcare for Barrett. I had to stay alert and levelheaded to discuss options with the surgeons that would affect my family forever. My family couldn't afford for me to be weak, so I decided I would have to dig deep and remain strong to keep us together.

Months later, my intuition about the seriousness of this day was revealed. Matt's hospital records confirmed that he had to undergo resuscitation serval times while going to the OR. The feelings of losing my husband that day were real, but God had other plans and gave him another day to fight.

For the next two days, Matt did not have any surgeries scheduled. They wanted to give his body a chance to heal before they went back in to check his vascular system. He still needed blood transfusions, but not nearly as many as the first four days. When Matt was unconscious, I spent almost eighteen hours a day in his room. I spent most of these hours alone, which wasn't always bad. It was exhausting having to constantly talk to and update Matt's status.

It was nice to take a walk down memory lane. I found I treasured the little things about our lives the most, the things we both took for granted. My hope was that constantly hearing my voice would wake him up.

Maybe my eyes were playing tricks on me, but when I told him the story of our engagement, I swear I witnessed him crack a brief smile.

FLASHBACK

June 2013

This is that story. Matt and I drove to Atlanta, Georgia, for our friends T-Bob and Caitlin Hebert's wedding. They were two of our best college friends. Matt played football with T-Bob, and I spent many Saturdays tailgating with Caitlin cheering on our boyfriends. I was one of Caitlin's bridesmaids, and we were looking forward to a fun-filled weekend with friends. Because everybody was fresh out of college, we split a hotel room with three other people. I could never imagine doing this now, but money was tight, and we would be partying all weekend, so it didn't bother us.

Matt was acting a little strange on the drive. He kept asking me about my future plans. I wondered why he was asking me these types of questions, but I figured he was just being goofy old Matt. We had been dating for the last six years, having met in high school, and dated through most of college, and marriage had come up in discussion, but I didn't think he was ready. I knew Matt very well, and he wasn't much for deep conversation. He tended to decide things on his own without wanting input from others.

I didn't have a concrete plan in place for my future, but I knew I wanted him to be a part of it. He really caught my attention when he asked, "Would you marry me?" I laughed it off and responded, "Well, yeah. What's with all the questions?" I had a feeling something was up.

They had a beautiful wedding with an incredible band, delicious food, and all our friends were there. The wedding was decorated with all things Louisiana. The first line dance was a tribute to New Orleans Mardi Gras, followed by an appearance from Mike, the tiger, the costumed mascot, not the real tiger.

T-Bob had requested coconut shrimp, and I watched Matt eat about two trays of them by himself. Matt was sort of keeping his distance from me at the reception. He hurt my feelings by doing this, and I wondered if I had done something wrong.

Toward the end of the night, it came time for the bouquet toss. All my friends kept looking at me and smiling. Two of them grabbed me and put me right in the middle of the front row of girls. I thought they were just trying to get me in a good spot to catch the bouquet so they could give Matt a hard time about getting married. Yeah, this is a great idea; I thought I would love a little payback for him being a jerk all night.

The band took its place, and Caitlin walked out about ten feet from the girls. She turned her back to us, then started acting like she would throw the bouquet. Each time she pump-faked, the band's drummer would play a ba da da boom! Ba da da boom! Ba da da boom! After a couple of times, she turned around and walked straight in my direction. With a big smile on her face, she handed me the bouquet. I looked at her in confusion until I saw Matt walking toward me out of the crowd and he got down on one knee.

My mouth dropped, and my hands went up to my face, softly slapping myself on the cheeks. I threw my head back and started laughing with joy and excitement. Matt was beaming as he asked me, "Will you marry me, Liana?" He held out the most gorgeous ring I had ever seen. I shook my head, yes, and everyone in the place went crazy, screaming and clapping. Matt swooped me up in his strong arms like a baby doll and twirled me around the dance floor.

It was a moment I will never forget. We danced while the band played Wagon Wheel by Darius Rucker. He explained how he and Caitlin had planned the proposal weeks earlier. So, this explained why he had been acting so strangely! I couldn't stop smiling or staring at my beautiful ring all night. Finally, I was going to marry this man I loved so much.

CHAPTER 8
Answered Prayers

I prayed to God every day that he would continue to allow Matt to progress. After each prayer, I told Matt he also had to pray. I reminded him to tell God he needed more time on earth. I wouldn't take no for an answer. Why I thought I could tell God what to do or I knew what was best seems a little silly now. God had a plan for this all along.

Late one night, I glanced at a folder and noticed the words cardiac arrest. I quickly pulled the paper out of the folder and read something along the lines of cardiac arrest upon arrival. Haley and I discussed this, so we decided to ask the nurse on the schedule that day if he knew more. He returned later and said he couldn't find more details in Matt's file.

The anesthesiologist from Vicksburg, Dr. Welch, visited Matt a couple of days later in the Jackson ICU. During his visit, he casually mentioned to Matt's mom he believed Matt had been in cardiac arrest for around forty-five minutes on December 28th. I could not believe my ears when I heard this. How does anybody go through that trauma and survive? Although Matt had been through a lot, he still had a lot more to go through if we made it out of there.

My husband showed very few signs that he was mentally there to the hospital staff. They had seen him do a few head turns when asked, but they mostly saw him lying there unresponsive.

The concern started to surface that even if Matt did wake up, he could suffer from cerebral anoxia, a.k.a. brain dead. I couldn't believe or accept that was his fate.

Nurses would come into his room every day and speak to him loudly like they were trying to communicate with a person hard of hearing. "Matt, are you there? Can you move? Squeeze my hand. Can you wiggle your toes? Can you feel me touching your foot?" they would shout. Every time he lay there unresponsive to the nurses.

I swear he would respond to small things for me, but the nurses never saw any of it. This happened when I would tell him stories or play videos of Barrett laughing. His lip would quiver, and the corner of his mouth would rise ever so slightly like he was trying to smile. I was beginning to think that maybe my mind was playing tricks on me, and I imagined Matt doing these things. I would tell the nurses and doctors what I saw, but they would just shake their heads in disbelief.

On January 4th, the doctors ordered an MRI to evaluate for cerebral anoxia to see if it was even worth continuing to try and save Matt's leg. They were trying to allow him to be as mobile as possible by keeping as much of his left leg as possible. If he was brain dead, they would amputate the entire leg, making him a hip disarticulation. They explained he would most likely be in a wheelchair if this happened. I could never imagine Matt in a wheelchair. I believed he would grow angry and bitter if he woke up to that realization.

I prayed to God every day to save his life and allow him more time on this earth. But I began to wonder if these prayers were selfish. Would it really be best for him to live but be miserable? What if he could never accept his new reality and make a new life out of it? How would his anger impact Barrett? Could our marriage survive this?

I chose to keep my distance from the lobby as we waited for his MRI results. Emotions and tensions ran high. Everyone was discussing what my options were as his wife. What would life be like for Barrett and me if Matt's mental capabilities were gone?

I did not want everyone to know about the brain test. Family members were already losing hope because he had not woken up yet. Who knows what rumors would start to circulate if they heard the doctors were concerned about his mental capabilities? I felt I owed it to my husband to stay strong and keep fighting just as hard as he was to stay with us.

After an agonizing wait, we were informed there was a minor brain bleed, but overall, he had not lost any cognitive function. This was an absolute miracle. The doctors seemed at a loss for words on how this was possible. Medically, it was impossible.

We faced a complex surgery. Now that Matt's brain function was believed functional, the surgeon team wanted to get the best possible outcome for Matt's mobility. The muscle around Matt's rebuilt vascular system was continuing to die. This meant he was at continuous risk for an arterial blowout, which could very quickly end his life. The surgeons briefed me that they were weighing the pros and cons of going in and operating again.

There was a chance that more muscle would be necrotic and that more of the leg would need to be amputated. If more of the leg had to be taken, that meant all the surgeries spent to rebuild and keep Matt's vascular system would be lost. One step forward, ten steps back.

I felt this was an important decision and wanted Matt's parents to be involved. I asked the doctors if we could meet before the surgery took place that day. It's not easy to throw a meeting together with three different doctors. We dealt with a vascular surgeon, an orthopedic surgeon, and a plastic surgeon. They made it happen, and we were able to have a quick conversation.

The doctors brought up that Matt could develop antibodies to the blood transfusions during the brief meeting. Talk about feeling like you are on another planet. How was Matt's body now rejecting the blood keeping him alive? Suppose the blood given is different from your blood type. In that case, your immune system can develop antibodies and attack the foreign blood type. Matt had been receiving O-negative blood. They had to act fast after being shot because he had nearly bled out. The doctors also told us they didn't know if enough blood was available for the surgery.

Now there might not even be enough blood to keep Matt alive for the day.

I felt like I would throw up or pass out. Everyone was on the edge of their seat because there was so much at stake. We had no choice, though. The surgery had to be done. I signed more consent forms and went to the lobby to figure out how to get more blood for Matt.

People came from far and wide to donate blood for Matt. Our family and friends organized blood drives throughout Louisiana and Mississippi. Matt used up copious units of blood, but his story got people out to donate more blood. One blood drive in Sterlington, the town we attended high school, donated 188 units in a single day! My friends Katie and Sam forced their way onto the Jackson local news show and pleaded for people to give blood. After their debut on the news, they stood on the side of the road, in the rain, waving a sign telling people where to donate blood for Matt.

I proudly told the nurses that we had raised more blood than Matt used of the hospital's resources. Life Share Louisiana later told us Matt set an unofficial record for the most blood donated in a person's name for our state.

Matt survived his seventh surgery in eight days. They described his vascular rebuild as sitting in soupy dying muscle. It was only a matter of time before we had real problems. At this point, seventy-five percent of his thigh had been removed.

After this surgery, Matt was still in a coma, but his body was making progress toward recovering. Fewer interventions were needed to keep him stable, and his body started to run without blood transfusions or pressers.

That night, I experienced a spiritual encounter that I will never forget. I had been sleeping in the recliner in Matt's room when I awoke to voices in the room and alarms going off. Doctors and nurses came into the room to assess Matt's state and what was causing his body to react negatively to the surgery. One nurse was doing a poor job of keeping a poker face. She paced nervously with her hand covering her mouth. I bolted in my chair upright, ready to face the catastrophe when I noticed their concern.

This is hard to put into words, but I became overwhelmed with fear as I sat in silence, scared and watching. I felt an evil presence come in and fill up every inch of space in the room. My heart began to pound as I struggled to breathe in the heavy, darkness-filled air. I had never felt a presence like this in my life. It felt like a spiritual battle between good and evil trying to take Matt. Nothing like this happened on any other night I stayed in the hospital. The nurse's faces looked puzzled and of grave concern.

I grabbed an Olive Wood holding cross Amy had given to me and began to pray. I prayed to God to make the dark presence leave and repeated over and over, "I do not fear evil. God is with me. God will protect us. Evil has no power over God." After chanting this in my mind, the heavy air in the room seemed to lift, the dark, evil feeling left, and Matt's machines began to steady. I truly believe God saved Matt that night. When I reflect on this, I know evil was ready to end this story and end the work God wanted to use through Matt.

CHAPTER 9

Clickbait

Matt's story spread like wildfire from local papers to ESPN with headlines reading, "Owner Shot by Dog" or "Former LSU Football Player Shot by Dog." I want to believe no ill intent was meant by the first stories, but it was hard to read. Some of the articles seemed to be more focused on saying something crazy or a clickbait title than the tragedy of the situation.

Then I would see the hurtful comments people would post. Matt would read this someday. It was hard for me to swallow that online articles were made without Matt telling his story first. He didn't get to think about it or prepare a statement. Everyone else did it for him, and he would have to live with the fallout.

Many articles got the details completely wrong, and nothing could be done about it. A lot is said about people's rights to privacy and having some sort of respect shown by the media, but I didn't see a lot of that. It was almost like some outlets were just glad to have a story like this to get more viewers or readers. Our tragic life was turned into clickbait.

I was very protective over my husband during his time in the SICU. I felt awful that he was going through this, and that he would wake up as an amputee. I knew Matt, and I knew how much he would struggle. He had always been very independent and physically active; his job even required him to be sometimes. Knowing that everyone would find out before he found out he was an amputee broke my heart.

But for every negative, there always seems to be a positive.

Good things came from Matt's story being picked up the way it was. A GoFundMe page had been started for people who wanted to donate money to help with Matt's medical costs. I assumed Matt's medical bills would be through the roof. As I started to do the math in my head, I realized we would be in debt for the rest of our lives. Everything was expensive; air evac, hospital stay, prosthetic leg, and home renovations. The list was endless. Matt was very money conscious. When he woke up and realized the debt we would be in, I feared that might send him back into cardiac arrest.

However, God was looking out for us. At one point not too far into this ordeal, close to 1,000 people had donated over $90,000 to us through GoFundMe. I couldn't believe that people were so generous to our family. Donations came from friends and family, but many came from complete strangers. People saw we were in need, and people came to help. So, even though the stories and comments were tough to read, good did come out of it. God used Matt's story to reach people, and he is still using it today. We will gladly pay it forward for the rest of our lives.

On January 7th, before I could enter the room to visit Matt, I had to put on a hazmat suit. This was traumatic as well. Not just the fact that it seemed so crazy but that his situation was so serious that it required something like this. Amazing. Due to his lab readings, they believed Matt had contracted clostridium difficile, a bacterium that could cause me to have mild to life-threatening diarrhea. This type of news didn't even faze me at this point. I had seen and experienced things over the last eleven days that I did not know were humanly possible. I was numb to any kind of shock. It was just kind of, "Okay, what's next?"

As I sat there looking like I had just returned from a spacewalk, I watched my unrecognizable husband and longed for a time when this would not be my reality. Why did I let Matt stay at the camp that second night? I could have told him he needed to come home.

A couple of hours later, the nurse popped her head in the room and gave me the all-clear on their clostridium difficile concerns. I didn't have the energy to go through the effort of taking off the overkill gown and gloves, and I could barely keep my eyes open. I just wanted my husband to wake up and tell me everything would be okay.

Later that day, the nurse brought in a pair of brain electrodes. She put them on Matt's head to stimulate his brain and assess his cognitive function. He slightly responded to the electrotherapy, but he did not wake up.

CHAPTER 10
Be Careful What You Wish For

On January 8, a day that we were praying and hoping for happened. Matt finally woke up. It was a miracle . . . again.

It had been twelve days since the accident. When I left to eat lunch, Matt's mom Brenda went for a visiting hour from noon to 1 p.m. I was so excited that I could hardly eat, and I was smiling for the first time in days.

Matt's breathing tube was still in when I got back in the room, and he was mad. His eyes were wide open, and he was mouthing angrily, "Get this thing out!"

Matt was furious that neither one of us would nor could help him. The nurse finally came to remove the tube. When I heard his voice, I about jumped on top of him. I leaned on him, kissed his cheek, and put my hands on his face. In classic Matt fashion, he responded in an aggravated tone, "Cold hands! Get them off!" This was not the first interaction I had been dreaming about. However, these words were so monumental! We knew his brain hadn't suffered from lack of oxygen, but that didn't mean he would come back the same.

These words let me know instantly my husband was back. This was precisely something Matt would say and just how he would say it.

You imagine that moment as full of tears, and "I love you," but his body was reacting to the trauma he had been through. He was shaking uncontrollably, cold, confused, heavily medicated, and starving. Nothing terribly significant happened during that lunch visiting hour. His mom and I mostly listened to Matt ask for water, ice, or blankets, and I don't remember saying a whole lot. I just watched him almost like a zoo animal. I was nervous to say too much because I didn't want to upset him with bad news. I mostly let him lead the talking.

After the lunch visiting hour, Brenda left, and it was just Matt and me. This was an interesting and exhausting afternoon. He wanted food so badly. The problem was he was only cleared for an ice chip diet and minimal water until the speech therapist could come to examine his throat. We had no idea when this would be, so I had to tell Matt over and over," No. You can't have food." This would infuriate him, and he would say I was such a rule follower. I didn't like him being angry with me. I was only trying to do what was best, but I knew it was the pain, trauma, and medicine talking. So, Matt would beg and beg for more water. I would remind him he could only take tiny sips out of the straw.

In stubborn Matt fashion, he would put the straw in his mouth and start sipping slowly, then when he had my trust, he would slurp as fast as he could, so I wouldn't have time to pull the cup away. He would finish the whole cup of water in about two seconds. That only kept him satisfied for five minutes at a time before he was back begging for food. This is a man who loved to eat and wasn't used to hearing the word "no." And I know he was truly starving for something to eat.

Matt began to obsess over his left leg.

Because of phantom pain and the medication, Matt didn't realize his leg had been amputated. He could sense something was wrong, but he had no idea it was gone. He never lifted the covers to look. He would ask things like, "Where is my left boot? I need my left boot. Will you scratch my left leg? My left leg hurts." He asked the questions repeatedly, and his tone was not innocent; it seemed almost like he was being an intentional jerk. He would look me in the eyes like he was challenging me. It was almost as if he knew his leg was gone but wanted to see if I was brave enough to say it.

This was tough. I was torn and a little frustrated at Matt's behavior for giving me such a hard time. But the circumstances were completely insane. I tried to ignore it and be understanding. Even more difficult, I would sit in silence and contemplate how to tell him his leg was amputated and predict how he would act. I was terrified. What if he started screaming and yelling, and we couldn't get him under control? What if his reaction was complete hysteria, and they sedated him again?

I decided to get the nurse's opinion. I told the nurse the questions Matt had been asking and asked him if he thought it was okay if I broke the news. He recommended that I go ahead and tell him so he could begin to process it. Could I do that? Dare I do that? I was still scared. This wasn't the time to make a critical mistake, and I certainly didn't want to make one. I went back to Matt's room and lightly said, "Matt, there was an accident, and your left leg was hurt very badly."

I left it at that, and Matt continued to quiz and question me. That's all I dared to say. I didn't want to be the reason none of his family could see him for the rest of the day. He was already mad, and I didn't want him to hate me, even if he really didn't mean it. I'd been through a lot, but I wasn't sure I could handle that at this point. I called Mark close to the 5 p.m. visiting hour and briefed him on his son's behavior. I told him that I had not fully explained what had happened.

Now that he was awake, the UMMC SICU staff got to see the real Matt, and boy was it hysterical. He has always had a playful personality and could get anybody laughing. Take that and the massive amounts of pain medicine in his system, and you had an endless supply of entertainment. He refused to give up begging for food. I asked Dr. Joe if there was any way around this, but safety trumps patient appetites. Dr. Joe explained to Matt that waiting was in his best interest.

Matt said something back in a sassy tone along the lines of, "So y'all are just going to let me starve? I need some nutrition."

Dr. Joe made a comment back something along the lines of, "Well, when you've been under sedation so long, it is in your best interest to let your throat heal, so there aren't any issues." The doctor said it in an aggravated tone and let out a mocking laugh.

Matt glared at the doctor and began to laugh, mocking the doctor, and then abruptly stopped and gave him a soul-piercing glare of hatred.

It was hilarious, and I tried not to giggle out of respect, but it was so funny. Matt was much easier for them to deal with asleep versus awake.

Matt then hallucinated and told me that doctors and nurses were taunting him with food. He kept looking at his IV bag rack, begging me to hand him the ice cream. He lashed out at the hospital staff and said things like, "If you are supposed to be taking care of me, then why are you throwing food at me? What kind of hospital is this? Y'all have a lot to learn!"

It was rather hilarious to see and hear some of the things he did and said. Frankly, I was just so glad to see him doing things and saying things like Matt. The staff, of course, was used to this type of behavior from patients. How he treated the staff depended on how they responded to his outrageous request. He took it easy on them if they would entertain him and play along. If they mocked him or refused his demands, he would give them hell.

For example, Matt hated the breathing treatments. He had to have them because he came down with pneumonia while in a coma. I never understood why he dreaded the breathing treatments so much. All he had to do was lay there and breathe into a mask. Whichever nurse would administer the treatment had to deal with the wrath.

One nurse was not in the mood for Matt's antics. He was a little abrupt and forceful with the mask. Matt put the mask on and very drastically yanked it off. He looked at the nurse and said, "Man! Did you wipe your butt with this? It smells horrible! You're disgusting, dude!"

Days later, Matt was finally cleared for a liquid diet. I had eyed a Smoothie King across the street, and when he got the green light, I literally sprinted there. I was running so fast that I nearly tripped five times. Trying to run in well-worn UGG boots is not easy. I was excited, and my adrenaline was pumping full throttle. I couldn't believe I was getting a smoothie for my husband. He was indeed alive!

I returned to Matt's room with a large size thirty-two-ounce chocolate high protein smoothie at record speed and proudly handed it to him. I would have gotten a sixty-ounce if they had such a thing. Looking back, this rich smoothie may not have been the best choice for him at the time. I probably should have gone with something a little lighter and smaller. When he took that first sip, a single sizeable heartfelt tear slowly rolled down his cheek. Oh, my goodness. It was the most pitiful thing I had ever seen. I don't remember, but I'm sure I cried a tear of joy or two myself.

I was so glad my husband was finally awake. The twelve days leading up to this felt like twelve months of waiting to have my Matt back. I felt like I could breathe and see a future past this awful nightmare. I didn't care that he was giving me a hard time. In my mind, he had earned it! I was grateful for every second I got to see him awake, alive, and talking.

The road ahead of us had so many unknowns, and these unknowns kept me awake at night. I'd focused all my energy on wanting Matt to live. Now it was time to figure out how we would live. I knew we were at a crossroads, where our next steps would decide the outcome of the rest of our lives. We could let this confine and control us or overcome this and learn to appreciate our life that had changed in ways we never imagined. This, too, was overwhelming, but I knew we had to try to work through it.

The doctors considered Matt's survival and waking up with full cognitive function medically impossible. A person who goes through the number of surgeries, blood loss, and cardiac arrest that Matt went through just does not survive. Doctors called Matt's survival a miracle, beyond a miracle, and I agree.

Here are a few strange occurrences that allowed my husband to live. When one minor thing could have tipped the scales against his survival, amazing things went his way that are beyond explanation.

Because Matt had fallen in the icy waters that morning while duck hunting, his blood vessels had contracted enough to slow his blood loss down to get him to the hospital in time. His friends' simple decision to take him to the highway versus back to camp allowed Matt to get to the hospital twenty minutes faster. At that moment, every second counted. The highway had a steep embankment, and they laid Matt's head on the downhill side, allowing blood to rush to his head, oxygenating and saving his brain. Nobody there that day was a medical professional. They had no idea how they laid my husband is exactly the procedure used in the hospital when a patient goes into cardiac arrest. Thank you, David Joe and Micah.

The doctors at Vicksburg had already put a patient to sleep for an elective surgery before Matt's arrival. Matt arrived just before they began to operate on the patient, so they were able to wheel them out of the OR so they could start to operate on my husband immediately. Even though Matt stayed in cardiac arrest for an extended period, thank God, the nurse in Vicksburg never stopped doing CPR, allowing oxygen to flow to his brain.

Dr. Welch, the anesthesiologist at Vicksburg, shared his story with Brenda when he checked on Matt at UMMC days later.

Dr. Welch's Story

When your son came in, we didn't have much hope. He had lost a lot of blood, and we had seen this type of accident many times before. Most people do not survive these types of injuries. After your son coded for forty-five minutes, I had finally given up hope and was headed back to my office upstairs. Before getting to my office, they called and told me that they had miraculously revived him! I immediately picked up the phone to call UMMC, which was where he needed to get to quickly. I tried to reserve a bed for him and discovered their ICU had no open beds.

Fortunately, and miraculously for Matt, my son was one of the department heads in the UMMC ICU. I called him and explained the situation. He was able to pull strings to make a bed available. When I called Air E-Vac out of Natchez to transport Matt, they told me they couldn't fly due to the weather. The clouds were too low to get flight clearance. I pleaded with them to find a way because Matt would die. After begging and pleading, they agreed to attempt the transport.

I was waiting on the helipad and could hear the chopper but could not figure out where they were coming from. It was that cloudy. Out of the gray sky, they finally appeared from the north. They ended up flying west into Louisiana and up into Arkansas and entered Vicksburg from the north. The minute they landed, the heavy clouds lifted and gave them a safe straight shot to Jackson.

The surgeons on staff that first night in UMMC were the exact surgeons Matt needed for his injury. Later, they explained how rare it was for all of them to be there at that time, especially on a Friday between Christmas and New Year's.

Matt was given over 300 units of blood.

This is an insane amount, and he needed every drop of it to stay alive. It is a miracle there was enough O-negative blood supply to keep him going for over two weeks. The synchronicities that happened that day make my mind race.

Some days of recovery, I felt hope that we were moving forward. Other days I felt trapped in pity and sorrow for our new way of life. Matt and I had to lean on one another through the good and bad. I gave it when Matt felt like giving up and needed tough love, and Matt reassured me it would be okay when I was overcome with worry.

It felt like us against the world. No one could understand the physical, emotional, and mental mountains we faced. Matt could've let his amputation tear apart our family marriage and destroy our lives. He didn't do that. Instead, he chose to fight. He chose to live. He chose to rise above his circumstance. I thank God every night for Matt's fighting spirit.

CHAPTER 11
Good Drugs

Matt

When I woke up on January 8th, I didn't know where I was. While I was in a coma, I had dreams that were so vivid I was convinced they really happened. I thought I had been out living life and had been brought in for surgery that day. I remembered I had been shot, but I had no clue what my body had been through the past twelve days.

The first person I remember seeing was my mom. She was smiling and seemed very happy, so I became happy too. Minutes later, Liana walked into the room. She was also smiling and happy.

As I looked around the room, I noticed odd things taking place. The room was a bright white, and all kinds of strange sounds came from behind me. The only parts of my body that could move were my eyes and mouth. And I was moving both of those profusely. The strangest thing I noticed was the clock on the wall. Each time the minute hand moved, it would suddenly spring off the wall, bounce around for a couple of seconds, and then stop. Then there were these two big water tanks positioned on opposite sides of the room. Water was flowing through a cluster of clear pipes from one tank to the other.

I was facing a wall of bookshelves. The shelves were shuffling up and down, left and right, in a strange hard-to-comprehend pattern. Every so often, I would catch a glimpse of somebody moving behind the shelves. When I would close my eyes, I saw brightly colored strange shapes and faces.

As the nurses came in to check on me, I gave them all a nickname. One male nurse walked in; I lit up and tried to figure out who he looked like, "I know, I know." I said, "You look like that country singer, um, that good-looking guy, um, oh yea, Luke Bryan!" I don't know if he appreciated or was offended by my comparison, but I didn't care. His name will always be Luke Bryan to me.

The nurses were startled by my behavior when I woke up. I had been quiet and motionless for twelve days, and now I wouldn't shut up.

I noticed that my left leg was itching very badly. I begged people to scratch, move it, or anything. All I got were blank stares. I couldn't move my arms, legs, or head. I was basically paralyzed, and I didn't know why. The pain meds were my friend and would continue to be my friend for the rest of my stay. They were also most likely the source of my vivid dreams and wild behavior.

The timeline in my head was a little skewed. I knew I had surgery because I had been shot, but I thought I only had one, and I would go home soon.

In one of my vivid dreams that I believed to be real. I was considering leaving Liana for another girl. The only reason I was considering this was that the girl's dad was worth $300 million. I didn't know if Liana knew any of this, and I half expected her to slap me at any minute.

I had other dreams, and I was upright, walking around in them. So, when I woke up and thought all my dreams were, in fact, real, I believed the leg that was shot was okay.

Quickly, hunger pains started to set in, and I asked for food. I didn't care what kind of food, I was so hungry anything would do. I begged every nurse who walked through the door to feed me, and every one of them said no. After what I thought to be an eternity of begging, I began to turn downright mean and started making nasty threats. I would threaten to talk to their boss and write hateful messages on their Facebook wall. But no matter what I said, the nurses continued to hold their ground. This was just the beginning of my battle for food.

A couple of hours later, my mind was taken off food.

I suddenly realized I had to poop, and there was no way I could get out of bed. I screamed, "I have to poop!" as loud as I could, hoping I would quickly catch a nurse's attention.

A male nurse poked his head and shoulder through the door frame and said, "Just go, man."

I gave him a wild-eyed look and asked, "In the bed?"

He nodded and explained I had a tube jammed up my butt that would catch the poop. So, I listened, and I went. Well, pooping in a tube that was jammed in my butt was a first for me. I wasn't sure how it was supposed to feel, so I just went for it. It was a pleasant sensation at first, but that soon changed.

I started to yell, "I think something is wrong!"

The nurse popped back in and said, "You're probably fine."

I said, "No, I think you need to check it. Something doesn't feel right."

Annoyed, he rolled his eyes and walked over to the possibly toxic bed. When he threw the course bed sheets back, his upper lip curled. Apparently, when I was pooping, the tube slid out of my butt, and poop was all over my now disgusting bed. He turned around and left my room. I thought to myself, "Is he just going to leave me like this?" Minutes later, he returned with a red bucket and two male nurses.

Since the poop got all over the bed and me, they had to change my sheets and clothes. Two guys would have to pick me up to do this while the other one changed the sheets. We went over the game plan, and they all took their positions. One . . . two . . . three . . . As soon as they lifted me up, pain coursed through my entire body. I screamed and told them to hurry. I had never felt pain like that in my life. It felt like ten guys were beating me with baseball bats all at once.

They worked as fast as possible, and I was soon relieved from the intense pain. I lay still for a couple of seconds to take deep breaths. When they finished cleaning up, they asked if I was alright. I said, "I'm fine. Is that all y'all got?" All three smiled and left the room. I would become known among the nurses for my sense of humor.

Just as my hunger pains came back, Liana and one of the other nurses appeared in my room. They were carrying an ice cream machine and a bag of toppings to go with it. I quickly perked up and started salivating. I asked, "Is all that for me?" like a kid being handed their first snow cone.

Liana and the nurse kept glancing out the door and were moving around stealthily. They explained how I wasn't supposed to have any food, but they felt bad for me and decided to get me some anyway. They made me promise I wouldn't tell any of the other nurses or doctors about this because they could get in serious trouble. I promised and sat there with a giant grin from ear to ear.

Before they could hand me any ice cream, there was a noise in the hallway and they both bolted. Just as she left the room, Liana looked back at me and whispered, "Be right back." I thought to myself, "Okay, they just don't want to get caught."

So, I lay there and waited patiently. After a couple of minutes, I became concerned that the delicious ice cream would melt. My patience started to wear thin, and my mood was turning sour.

More minutes went by, and I got downright mad. They left the precious ice cream where I could see it, so I had to watch in disbelief as it melted away. "That's it. I've had enough," I thought to myself. I started to whimper like a puppy, and I was fighting back the tears. "Why do they have to do me this way? Don't they know I can't reach the ice cream?"

This went on for an hour before Liana showed back up. I lit into her, "How could you do me this way? You know how hungry I am! You are torturing me!"

She gave me a blank look and said, "What are you talking about?"

"The ice cream! You just left it here to melt!" I replied.

She said, "What ice cream?"

I cut my eyes to where I thought it was, and it was gone. "Where did you put it?" I screamed.

She said, "Matt! I have no idea what you're talking about."

"So that's how you want to play this? Fine!" I said.

People were constantly in and out of your room when you are an ICU patient. Every five minutes, somebody would come in, stick me with a needle, ask me questions, and leave. This was all brand new to me the first night after snapping out of my twelve-day coma. I quickly became aggravated with all the foot traffic.

Soon it was time to get a little sleep. I became so utterly cold I started shaking uncontrollably. I made them pile at least seven blankets on top of me that first night. Liana stayed with me in my room. It's a good thing she is small because the so-called bed she had to curl up on was leaning to the right old broken recliner, which caused her aggravating neck pain.

The hospital after dark is a strange place. I fell asleep quickly, but I didn't stay asleep long. When I woke up, I noticed a pair of yellow eyes peering at me from behind the shelves in my room. I quickly closed my eyes for fear that someone was spying on me. When I opened my eyes again, they were gone. My eyes began to gaze around the room when suddenly I noticed a skeleton man standing behind the door. At first, I was frightened. I whispered to Liana, "Do you see that?" but she was sound asleep. So, I looked back at the skeleton and noticed it was just a skeleton used for medical school students to learn about bone structures. "Whew," I thought, "it wasn't a real skeleton man."

I noticed one of the shelves moved, and suddenly I was sprayed with water. "Hey!" I yelled out, "Quit messing with me." I heard people giggle behind the shelves, and I realized I was being pranked. "Haha, okay, very funny," I said.

I glanced back toward the creepy skeleton man, and he had moved closer to my bed. His arm was now stretched out while holding a giant slice of pepperoni pizza in his hand. Oh, man, did that piece of pizza look good. I was still not allowed to eat anything, and my hunger pains were barking. "It's those people behind the shelves; they are getting a kick out of torturing sick patients," I thought. I was so mad at this point. I decided I would close my eyes and try to tune them out.

Shortly after I closed my eyes, I heard an abrupt noise coming from the side of the room my window was on. I opened my eyes and saw a nurse opening a secret door and handing pills to a sketchy-looking person standing outside. "Wait, is she dealing drugs out of my hospital room?" I tried to play it cool and act like I was asleep so she wouldn't notice me watching her. "Wow," I thought to myself, "I just discovered a drug-dealing ring right here in the hospital. She is probably selling my pills too! I will tell the doctors in the morning, and I bet she will be fired." I wondered if Liana knew any of this was going on. I glanced over at her, and she was asleep.

I could hear the faint sound of music playing on the floor above me. At first, it was tolerable, but it soon grew louder. It became so loud that I assumed the whole hospital could hear it, and the staff would tell them to shut it down. Well, the music kept playing, and I grew impatient.

I started to notice people moving around through the cracks in the ceiling. I wondered what they were doing up there. Suddenly two teenage kids bolted past my door, running down the hall. "Oh man," I thought, "they are having a camp for kids here right now. That's why the music upstairs is so loud." Oh, I was highly annoyed.

I looked back up at the cracks in the ceiling, and I could see a kid looking down at me. Suddenly I felt a white powdery substance falling on my face. It was getting in my eyes and nostrils. I started to yell, "Stop! Stop! I can't see!" I quickly closed my eyes, and what I saw was terrifying. Before me were demon-like creatures dancing in a ball of fire, grinning at me and moving closer. I would open my eyes, and the powder would fall back in. I closed my eyes, and the demons crept closer still. "Make it stop! Make it stop!" I yelled. I reopened my eyes, and the powder was gone. The music had stopped, and there was no sign of any kids. I wanted so badly for this night to be over with.

I must have dozed off for a spell when suddenly I was awakened. The drug-dealing nurse was back! She tried to open the secret door when her mother stepped in from the hall.

"I told you to stop doing this," her mother said. She walked over to her daughter, and they had a hushed conversation. I played possum again and tried to pick up on what they were whispering. I fully intended to turn the nurse in the following day. I had my heart set on it. I glanced back over at Liana, and she was still asleep. "Man, she is missing good stuff here," I thought. The nurse and her mother talked for what seemed to be five minutes, then left the room. I lay there planning how I would reveal the drug ring the next morning, and I must have fallen asleep.

A couple of doctors walked into my room early the following morning. I began to tell them about my horrible night. I let them know I didn't appreciate how I was being treated and explained what had happened in my room overnight. I told them that I demanded an apology from the kids who poured powder on me, and they also had a serious problem with one of the nurses stealing pills and selling them out of a secret door in my room. They gave me a blank stare, nodded their heads, and said, "Okay, we are sorry." Then they folded up their notepads and left.

A couple of days later, I realized all of these were hallucinations. Even the story of Liana and the ice cream was a wild hallucination. I would still have minor hallucination spells for days. Still, none were as intense as those I experienced the first night after I awoke from my coma.

This was not the first time I had had wild hallucinations in my life.

FLASHBACK

August 2010

The next day was an early morning practice at LSU. It was one of the first practices in full pads, and the whole team was combined as a single unit. The practices were split up in fall camp to give the incoming freshmen reps to learn calls and plays. We were used to it being hot in south Louisiana, but it was scorching on this day.

The practice was set up to be a long one. There were thirty-two scheduled periods, which was a lot. We started off the day with everybody healthy, but that soon changed.

I was having a good day. I had made excellent run blocks I knew would look great on film. I also had a good pass blocking day, which was not typical for me. I thought I had gotten my swagger back, and I was ready to make a push for a starting position.

Midway through practice, the first and second-string RGs went down on back-to-back plays. Coach Stud moved me over to the right guard to fill in for the rest of the grueling practice.

I ran first and second-team plays for the back half of practice without a break in between. After a couple of series, I was gassed. Our practices were fast-paced, and I barely had time to take a sip of water. I even refused to drink water through a couple of periods because I didn't have the energy between reps.

After the last scripted play, Coach Miles' squeaky voice yelled, "Behind the line!" Immediately everybody let out a big sigh because this meant perfect sprints. Perfect sprints meant that every team member had to break down, not jump offsides and run full speed through the line. If one player did not do so, the sprint didn't count.

The assistant coaches were positioned around the field to make matters worse, watching our every move. If they saw a player fail to do one of those things, they would call him out, and the team would berate the player with harsh insults while hurling water bottles in his direction.

When I got in line to run, I didn't feel quite right. I had a tough time catching my breath, and my body temperature felt hot. As we started to run the sprints, my legs felt rubbery, and I had trouble focusing. I nearly got in a fight with 53 because I was leaning and pushing on him. He turned around and hollered, "Get off me!" clenching his tiny fist, ready to deck me. But I couldn't help it. I felt horrible, and everything was starting to spin out of control. After three or four penalties, we finished the ten perfect sprints, and Coach Miles called the team up to take a knee.

When I knelt, I was in awful shape. I was breathing heavily, and it felt as if I had hot coals in my shoulder pads. I was panting like a dog and starting to wheeze. Other players gave me funny looks and handed me bottles of water. I quickly dumped the water and ice in my shoulder pads, trying to put out the imaginary hot coals I felt next to my skin.

After about ten minutes of Coach Miles rambling about practice, he told everybody to stand up so we could break it down. When I stood up, the world around me started to spin. I had my Riddell helmet clinched in hand after we broke it down. I took awkward steps toward Coach Stud, picked my purple and gold helmet up over my head, and slammed it to the ground. After that startling gesture, I began to laugh uncontrollably and stammer around in a crooked circle. Coach Stud yelled for the trainers. I was still laughing uncontrollably when our two head athletic trainers Shelly and Jack grabbed me by my arms. I laughed the whole way into the training room and continued to laugh as they took my pads and clothes off. After they got my gear off and recorded my temperature, they took me back outside under the awning, where they had an ice tub ready. They quickly put me in the water and poured buckets of ice on top of me.

By this time, coaches had made their way over to me. I was very loopy and hallucinating. I looked at the ceiling and thought it resembled a treadmill track running at full speed. I said, "The ceiling looks like a treadmill, haha!" The coaches glanced up, then looked back down at me, concerned, and confused.

Coach Moffitt started asking me questions. "Hey Branch, what goes good with ice?"

I replied, "BEER, Coach! Beer goes good with ice!"

They got a chuckle out of my answer, but this was no laughing matter. I was having a heat stroke right there before their eyes. After fifteen minutes in the ice tub, they got my body temperature back down to a more normal level. They took my temperature inside after getting my pads off. It was 106 degrees Fahrenheit. This was a significant heat stroke level!

Once I was back inside, they laid me down and hooked me up to an IV. My body was drained, and I was shivering. I was still a little loopy, and I was saying outrageous stuff. The players came by to check on me. I think I gave everybody a good scare when I was being escorted off the field while laughing uncontrollably like the Joker from Batman.

When your body reaches temperatures that high, your muscle starts to break down. They ruled me out of practice for the rest of the week for precautionary reasons. I was glad that I would get to take a break for a couple of days, but another part of me was upset that I had let myself reach that point. I should have noticed when my body started to feel off and taken myself out. But instead, I tried to be Mr. Tough Guy and fight my way through it. Now I would have to miss a bunch of reps, which would make it that much harder to earn a starting spot. I was also aggravated because I felt like I had put together my best camp practice so far. Instead of building on top of that, I had to let my body recover. Shelly told me my episode was one of the biggest scares she had experienced in her medical career.

CHAPTER 12
Tough News

I had zero strength left of what remained of my body. It is shocking how fast your strength disappears if you don't use it. I had to have a nurse or family member help me with everything for the first week. You don't know what helplessness is until you have someone feed you breakfast, lunch, and dinner for several days. Well, I guess this makes sense, I mean, I did come back from the dead more than once.

I still believed I had my left leg for a time. I kept asking people to scratch or rub it, but I received more blank stares.

I'll never forget my dad's visit that January day. My father's big frame walked through the door. He greeted me and sat down at the foot of my bed. He stared at the freshly mopped floor for a couple of minutes and took deep heavy breaths, trying to think of the words to say. I was a little confused about why he was acting so strangely.

"Dad," I said, "what's wrong?"

He looked up at me, and I noticed that he was crying. I have only seen my dad cry one other time in my life, and that was years ago when I was a kid. Strangely enough, that incident also involved a gun.

As he opened his mouth, I noticed his lips were trembling. He carefully said, "Son, they had to amputate your leg to save your life."

These words hit harder than a Mike Tyson combination punch to the face and the gut.

He said, "I love you, son. Your family loves you, and we are here for you to help get you through this. The most important thing right now is that you are alive, and you get to watch your son grow up."

I was speechless. How could this be? Because of my vivid comatose dreams, I thought I had been walking around just days ago. "What happened? I thought they fixed my leg after I got shot." These thoughts bounced around in my head for a while before reality sank in. "How does somebody move on after an amputation? I don't even know an amputee. Do I really want to live like this?"

I then looked up at my heartbroken father and said, "Okay, well, could you at least go get me some mac and cheese or something now, Papa?"

A cheerful smile went across my dad's face, and the thick air cleared the room. I'm not kidding; I was a clown when I had those pain meds on an IV drip. By no means was my dad nor I done thinking about my new life's challenges going forward. But I'm not one for sticky emotional conversations, so I countered him with a bit of humor.

I felt like life had sucker-punched me again. I had faced tough challenges throughout my short life, and time after time, I had found a way to overcome them. But this challenge would be like no other; I wasn't confident that I could get through this one. There was no quick fix, no simple solution. My leg was gone, and it would never come back.

Later that day, Liana was in the room with me. She talked on the phone to a surgeon for a very long time. I didn't understand what they were discussing, but I knew it was about me. After she hung up the phone, she explained their long conversation. She told me that the surgeons were concerned there was more dead tissue in what little remained of my left leg. She said they wanted to go back in and clean out the dead tissue before it became infected. The hope was that I could keep part of my leg. This would make it much easier to use a prosthetic, and my mobility challenges would be much less severe. She told me there was a chance I could lose all of my leg if there was too much dead tissue.

My revision surgery was set for the following day. That night Liana came to my room, and we prayed our hearts out that I would be able to keep what little bit of leg I had left. This was the only thing we knew to do. I felt like God owed this to me. "I've already lost most of my leg; now they want to take it all. Please say it's not so." I begged, pleaded, and bargained with God until I fell asleep that night.

The following day the surgeons came to my room to discuss the complicated surgery. They consulted with me about what they expected to find and the measures they would take to fix it. Basically, they told me they would probably have to take the rest of my leg. I told them that is not what I want to do, but the most important thing is that I stay alive. I explained how I trusted them to make the best decision.

They wanted me to understand the mobility challenges that would come with removing my entire leg. I said, "As long as I can climb in a tree stand, I'll be alright." One of the surgeons slightly cocked his head and eyebrow like he wasn't sure that would be possible. The surgeons stepped out into the hall and had a brief discussion before returning to the operating floor.

My dad was sitting in the corner, trying to digest the tough news. I could tell he was worried, so I told him I was okay with it. I trusted they would make the right call.

Over an hour later, a nurse came to wheel me to the OR. I was extremely nervous and nauseous. This was surgery number ten for me, but this was the first one of which I was aware. As they wheeled me through the doors, I got an excellent idea for a joke. They cleaned me up and transferred me over to the cold stainless steel operating table. They started sticking me with all kinds of needles connected to wires and tubes, and I soon looked as if I was lying at the bottom of a bowl of noodles.

When Dr. Hoppe walked in, I hit him with my spur-of-the-moment idea of a joke. I said, "Hey, if you do have to take the rest of my leg, do you think you might use some of that to add a few inches to my family jewels?"

He cracked a quick smile and said, “I’m glad to see you have a sense of humor about all this.”

Sadly, they ended up taking the rest of my leg. There was just too much dead tissue, and the risk of infection would have been too high.

CHAPTER 13
Same Story, Another Day

Each time they would give me anesthesia medicine for surgery, my hallucinations would come back with a vengeance. They were never as bad as my first night fresh out of comatose, but they did continue. For ten straight days after I woke up, I asked the nurses why they had moved me to a different room, even though I remained in the same room for all my twenty-five confusing days in the ICU. When I slept, I would have weird dreams about people I knew. I don't remember any details about these dreams, but I remember them being very strange.

They had me on a Dilaudid (hydromorphone) IV drip. This is a powerful pain medication. Its street name is drugstore heroin. Every ten minutes, a handheld button would light up green, which meant I could give myself another dose. It took me a couple of days to understand that there was a ten-minute timer, so I was punching that button like I was playing Jeopardy. Once I understood the timer, I would watch for the light like a drag racer, ready to hit the gas on the green.

My body quickly became addicted. Every morning I woke up feeling like I had been hit by a truck. This was because I had gone hours without the Dilaudid. I learned to wake up periodically through the night to dose myself. Still, my addiction became so bad that I would be in agony if I missed thirty minutes. I would wake up in the morning and hit that button every ten minutes on the nose, and after about four doses, I was back to feeling good. I called this my game time ritual. I even made Liana shoot a quick video of me explaining this odd behavior. This routine continued throughout my entire stay in the ICU.

I quickly grew tired of the overbearing ICU schedule. I would have two nurses every day, and it seemed like they lived in my tiny room. It was set up like this for a reason. I was a high-risk patient, and they took excellent care of me. I became friends with the nurses on the ICU floor. They would come into my room and watch football games with me and bring me snacks and purple popsicles from the kitchen. They treated me like a human being, not a sick patient. Their treatment helped me cope with my shocking new reality, and I will be forever grateful to all of them, more than I can say or that they will ever know.

Doctors would stop in every morning to see how I was doing. The first couple of mornings, they would walk in and seem surprised I was still alive. They told me they had never seen a case like mine where the patient lived and came back mentally sharp. I had done both of those things. The things they saw with me were previously considered medically impossible. They documented my case very well to share it with other surgeons and doctors around the country.

Although I was getting better, my vital signs were nowhere near normal. I still had a long way to go before being cleared to go home. My white blood cell counts were running high, and they feared my body was not done aborting tissue. If my counts did not come down, there was a possibility they would have to take part of my abdomen.

I tried to block these negative thoughts from my head and focus on getting my strength back. Per my request, a hospital physical therapist brought me a couple of stretch bands to do exercises while I lay in bed. I may have been the only ICU patient in history to request exercise equipment forty-eight hours after waking up from a twelve-day coma. I spent over an hour trying to tie the bands in various places on my bed to exercise different muscles. I was still weak, and my knots weren't perfect. Every so often, a band would come untied and would pop me in the hand or face. I'd yell and scream like I had been shot all over again, then sit and pout, even sometimes cry when this happened.

I thought about giving up nearly every second, but something burning deep inside me would not allow this to happen.

On January 17th, I woke up in intense pain. My residual limb was throbbing, and there was no amount of pain meds to make it stop. After lunch, the surgeons were called because my pain had gotten significantly worse. They decided to run a CT scan to see if they could find the cause of the problem. The CT scan yielded no results, so they decided to rush me into emergency surgery. By the time this decision was made, it was about 6 p.m.

Because I wasn't scheduled for surgery, I ate food all day. Since I had food in my stomach, they used a different method to put me under. When they gave me the medicine, my body had an allergic reaction, and my heart stopped beating for fifteen seconds. Amazingly, they got my pulse back, stabilized me, and finished the surgery. They ended up finding a baseball size hematoma in my residual limb, which was causing the throbbing pain.

This was surgery number eleven in twenty-one days. My body needed to start showing signs of improvement fast because the surgeons weren't sure how much more my heart could take.

My body was still holding fluid, and I had not been able to pass any urine thus far. My main goal was to move from ICU to the regular floor in the hospital. This was the next big step in my recovery. My kidney doctor was the only doctor who hadn't cleared me. This was because I could not pass urine. I had to be periodically hooked up to the dialysis machine to flush my body.

Against the doctors' medical advice, I decided to start drinking a lot of water. My hope was drinking the water would make me have to pee, and I could bust up out of ICU! Well, my thought to be a brilliant idea backfired. Instead, it overloaded my body. I held more fluid, and my potassium levels went through the roof.

My aunt, uncle, and cousin dropped by to visit me one day around lunch. During our visit, my nurse brought me a plate of food. All was fine as I started to eat, then suddenly I had to cough.

When I coughed, I vomited everywhere, all over my food and bed. This was all right in front of my family, and I was so embarrassed. These kinds of things are very dehumanizing. I couldn't hold my food down nor clean up after myself. This was worse than pooping myself in the bed, which I would save for other visitors.

I soon realized my water-guzzling was making things worse, so I changed my strategy. I basically quit drinking water, and I started to feel a little better. They hooked me up to the dialysis machine, and I felt immediate relief, but I still hadn't passed any urine to date. This was my current top priority. Day after day, they continued to use a catheter to drain my bladder, and day after day, I grew more impatient.

I hated the thought of someone else being in control of my destiny. I had been here before, and I now knew what it would take to overcome.

FLASHBACK

September 2010

Our first game was against North Carolina in Atlanta. It was one of those big-time televised non-conference games with hype and attention to kick off the season.

As a team, we felt good about the upcoming year. We had experience at key positions and talent all over the field. We went into opening week expecting to drum North Carolina. They had a very good defensive front, and Coach Stud pushed the offensive line hard the week before the game.

Things didn't start well as 60 went down with a nasty ankle injury during the first drive. Nobody knew at the time how bad it was, but we knew he would be out for the rest of the game.

Because it was in the middle of the drive, coach Stud put 53 in because he had the most experience. Coach did not want to risk 53 getting hurt because he was the backup center, and center was the hardest to replace, so he elected to put in the second-string right guard 74 on the second drive, and 74 was a monster of a human being. He was the biggest lineman on the team. He was also a very young player at the time, so the game's speed was still moving fast for him.

I walked up to the coach and told him that even though I played left guard, I felt like I could go in at right guard if needed. He nodded and went back to making calls for the game. Looking back, I think he was kind of upset with me because I didn't come forward with confidence and convince him that I genuinely wanted to go in the game.

We ended up beating North Carolina, and I played a chunk of the fourth quarter at left guard. After the game, we received word that 60 had broken his ankle and would probably be out for the remainder of the season. I remember when I heard this, I felt terrible for my buddy. He had worked hard in the offseason to win the starting job, and going down on the season's opening drive wasn't fair. Football can be a brutally unfair game. Kind of like life can be.

That following Monday, Coach Stud called the twos to visit him in his office. He told us that he was considering 74 and me for the starting spot at right guard that week against Vanderbilt. He said he wanted us to rotate every play with the ones in practice.

I was pumped when I got this news. I felt like I would finally get a chance to show what I could do in a game, and my fate rested in my own hands. Even though I was being considered to start that week, I approached practice the same as I always did. I was confident in my ability and knew I could get the job done.

Throughout the week, I received compliments from Coach Miles when I ran my share of plays with the ones and knew I had a good chance of starting. Thursday rolled around, and after practice began, Coach Stud told the special teams coach that 74 would be starting, so he would need to make adjustments. When I heard this, my heart sank a little. I was hoping I would get the nod to start that week because I felt good about my preparation and was a year older than 74.

Coach Stud never personally told me the news that he would start 74 over me, which bothered me a little. In all fairness, he did not owe me an explanation for his decision. It may have just been me, but I felt like he was mad at me in a way.

I ran all the plays with the twos that day, and it was the last practice in pads for the week. The next day was Friday, which meant walkthrough and travel. Since we played Vanderbilt in Nashville, and everyone expected to beat the tar out of them, most of the team would get playing time.

During the walkthroughs, Coach told me to let 74 take all the snaps with the ones. I tried not to let this bother me too much at the time. I still felt like I would get my chance to show what I could do on the field. I just needed to make sure I was mentally and physically ready when that time came.

When we landed in Nashville, we went straight to the stadium. Vanderbilt's stadium was not very impressive. Even worse, the visiting locker room was the size of my tiny high school locker room. But I thought to myself, "This is the place I will finally get my chance to show the coaches what I can do." I wouldn't let this unimpressive stadium dampen my good mood.

The offense had a film session the night before, and the Offensive Coordinator went through twenty-five plays. Each offensive position said out loud what their responsibility was. I chimed in on a few plays during that session, but 74 spoke on most of the looks. After the film session, we broke it down and headed out of the room to go to bed.

Coach Miles was sitting at the back of the conference room by the door. When I walked by, he pulled me aside and told me that he was excited to watch me play the next day and that I should make sure to get a good night's sleep. I enthusiastically nodded my head and said, "Sure thing, Coach!"

I was so pumped after the head coach said this to me. I knew that I would get my chance, and I needed to make the most out of this grand opportunity.

Because it was a night game, the team slept in, ate brunch, and went back to our rooms to rest. The team met back down in the lobby; everybody dressed in a coat and tie for our pregame meal and one more quick walkthrough. We were all crammed in that tiny locker room when we arrived at the stadium. It was no fun trying to get your gear on while rubbing shoulders with people on both sides.

Finally, it came time for the offensive line to hit the field for warmups. I felt a little sluggish when we ran out of the locker room. On our opening drive, 74 went in, and the offense drove the field's length for a quick score. On the second drive, 74 went back in the game and had the same result. At this point, I thought that, indeed, Coach was about to give me a series to see what I could do. In the next series, the same thing: 74 went in, and we drove the field and scored. Halftime came around, and I hadn't been on the field except for my role on special teams. But I didn't let it get me down. I knew I had to stay sharp for when my time came.

To start the third quarter, Coach put 74 back in the game, and we scored again. By this time, I thought to myself, "Okay, now what's the deal?" We had a big lead, and Vanderbilt didn't show any signs of making a comeback. But to my surprise, Coach put 74 back in the game on the next drive. The third quarter was ending by this time, and we had a sizable lead. Coach put the ones back in to start the fourth quarter, and yet again, they drove the field and scored. We were halfway through the fourth quarter with a more significant lead when our next drive came around.

Coach Stud called everybody up and said, "Okay, twos are going in this drive. I don't want to see any mistakes out there." At this point, I was aggravated. I wanted so badly to get in a series with the ones and show what I could do. Just before the drive, Coach Stud told me to stay on the sideline with him. "WHAT?!" I thought to myself. "What the hell is this about?! You aren't even going to put me in with the twos on this drive?" I was so mad I considered punching him right square in the face. It was now clear at this point that Coach was upset with me. I honestly had no idea what it could be. I practiced hard that week.

I was on time for all our meetings. What could I have possibly done to deserve this kind of treatment? The twos drove the field and scored while I sat on the sideline. I had to run in for the extra point after the score. As I was running off the field, Coach Stud was standing there high-fiving all the twos who had just completed the drive. I ran right beside him and purposely left him hanging. I was beyond mad at this point. I didn't understand how he could tell me he was considering me for the starting spot that Monday to not even put me in the game with the twos on Saturday. I could not figure out what I had done wrong.

After the game, I didn't say a word to anybody. The team was excited because we won the game, and the entire two-deep roster played, except for me. I took the short weekend and tried to get over my heartache. I didn't know what to do from here. I thought that maybe I should talk to Coach Stud and figure out what the deal was. Just ask him straight up what I did wrong and what I needed to do to correct it.

When Monday rolled around, I had it on my mind that I would ask him what had happened. We had our team meeting Monday morning. Coach Miles usually took key plays and broke them down for everybody to watch together. One of the plays was an offensive goal line snap, and he made it a point to highlight one of 74's blocks, complimenting him in front of the whole team. I remember thinking to myself, "Oh great, I will never get a chance now. Coach Miles just openly complimented my competition in front of everybody." He was for sure locked into the starting role for the upcoming game that week.

After the meeting ended, I thought about heading upstairs to talk to Coach Stud. I thought about it for a second and then decided I'd wait until later. I really needed to complete my first workout for the week before my classes started. I would go talk to him before practicing that afternoon.

I stretched, warmed up, and went about my usual routine of looking like I was working out while secretly skipping as many reps as possible. I had gotten very good at cutting reps in the weight room at that point in my career. I had convinced myself that I knew my body better than Moffitt, and I did not need to push myself to the limit during every workout. This soon became a tough habit to break, and I started secretly skipping at least thirty percent of the reps I was asked to do.

As I went through the workout, all the painful emotions from Saturday weighed heavily on me. I just couldn't figure out what I did wrong. The more I dwelled on it, the madder I got. I thought maybe he didn't think I was all in on the team. But wait, that couldn't possibly be the case. Everyone should have been aware that I was all in on the team since I had literally pushed myself to the edge during camp when I had a heat stroke.

As the day went on, these thoughts continued to consume me, but I did not stop by his office later that afternoon.

Moving on through the rest of the season, very little changed for my playing time. I never got any significant number of snaps with the ones, and I only got to go in on offense when we had a big lead. I never had that conversation with Coach Stud about my playing time, and I fell into a deep state of depression. I would lay in bed in my dark room all day before practice. I never went to class, and I hardly ate anything. I would get out of bed at 1:30 p.m. and head to Football Ops. I'd eat a protein bar and walk straight into the meeting room. Over the course of the season, I lost thirty pounds because I failed to take care of myself.

Sometimes I wish I could go back and kick my twenty-one-year-old self and tell him to swallow his pride and go talk to the coach. I have thought about this very moment at times throughout my life. I think about everything I did wrong and what I could have done to change it. I wish I had visited Coach Stud the week of the Vanderbilt game and watched the extra film with him. Maybe that's all he wanted me to do to show him that I cared. I have thought about this over the years, and to me, this was one of those moments where I had to make a choice at the crossroads.

If I could go back today, I would choose the road I didn't travel one hundred out of one hundred times. I think, what if I had gotten the nod to get the start that week? What would my life be like now? Would it be different? Better? Worse? I guess I will never know because there is no way to go back to find out. I must live with the choices I have made throughout my life, whether I like them or not.

CHAPTER 14
Liquid Gold

One glorious day in January, it happened. I grabbed my pee jug and held it in position. I closed my eyes and pictured a massive waterfall raining down from above. Then like riding a bike, it all came back to me. I had finally passed urine! I screamed for the nurse to come to see me and rejoiced like I had won the lottery! "I did it! I did it!" I yelled. The nurse didn't act too impressed. I had passed urine, but it was only an ounce or two. I didn't care how much it was; I now had confirmation that I could do it, and I knew efficiency would improve.

Seriously, I never thought I'd be gleeful over peeing in a jug. I would have probably laughed my head off at somebody telling such a story.

How very strange my life had become.

They told me to record the amount of urine I passed each time. This became a game to me, and I would win this game no matter what. I have never felt so much pride in my entire life than the pride I felt each time I filled up my pee jug.

Also, you need to understand that peeing in an odd-shaped plastic jug while lying flat on your back sick and nearly dead is not an easy task. I repeatedly spilled many drops of urine, and each time I would curse myself because I wouldn't be able to record that precious liquid gold.

Soon I began to dominate this game, and my kidney doctor, once my sworn enemy, became my friend. She told me that my numbers looked better, and I could be moved out of ICU soon.

Then the day came. My nurse told me they had a bed on the main floor. To me, it felt like I would imagine being called up to the big leagues! My dad was there that day to help me pack. I got him to snap a couple of pics of me in my ICU room before departure. Part of me was nervous about leaving. These people were my friends, and I knew the routine. They had taken such good care of me in the ICU that I would miss the staff. It felt like I was moving off to college all over again, excited, and nervous at the same time.

My room on the main floor was a significant upgrade. It was twice the size of my ICU room, and I had my own personal bathroom. The only thing lacking was the view from my window. It faced a solid brick wall, kind of what I would imagine a prison window view being. Later I would find this would turn out to be a good thing.

The nurse's schedule on the main floor was different. Gone were the days of somebody walking through my door every five minutes. Now they would only come if I called them. I would still have staff drop by a couple of times a day to bring me food and medicine, bathe me, and collect my urine jugs, but it was nowhere near the coverage I had on the ICU floor.

A physical therapist came by my room every day to get me up and moving. The first goal was to get me to sit up in bed. Once I had mastered that, they brought a wheelchair to my room. Freedom at last! Now I didn't have to sit in my room all day. I could get out and do a little exploring. They didn't know how dangerous I could be with this freedom!

I needed help the first day to transfer from the bed to the wheelchair. They made me promise that I would call a nurse and wouldn't attempt to do this on my own. I agreed only so they would leave the chair in my room. In my head, I was thinking, "I can do this by myself; it's not that hard."

Because the window view in my room was pitiful. I had to get in my chair and wheel myself down the hall to gaze out a big bay window overlooking the main entrance to the hospital. I would sit and watch all the people walking around, and I wondered if I would ever walk again. It just didn't seem fair that I was the one who had to go through this. I would sit and think, "Just look at all these people out walking around, not understanding how good they have it. What did I do to deserve this? Why not any one of them instead?"

Pushing the wheelchair around every day was good exercise, and my strength began to build. One day, a physical therapist brought a walker to my room and wanted me to practice standing up out of bed. I gladly accepted the challenge. I thought it would feel great to stand up since I had yet to do this. After a couple of attempts, I finally succeeded. It would not have been possible without two physical therapists spotting me and pulling me up. But all the same, I felt like I had done something big.

A couple of days went by, and I started to get the hang of standing up. My next task was to walk or hop with the walker for small steps across my room. I soon graduated to hopping with the walker a short distance down the hall. Each day I pushed myself to go a little further until I could go all the way to the bay window. Once I accomplished that distance, it was time to see myself in action.

My mom was there that day, so I asked her to record a little game film to watch and improve my form. I went all the way to the bay window, then turned around and made it all the way back to my room. This was the farthest I had hoped with the walker to date!

Once I laid back down in my bed, I pulled up the video on my phone. What I saw would tear me apart. I'll never forget the first time I saw the image of myself on that iPhone standing there with only one leg. I burst into tears, and all my insecurities cut me down to size. One-legged freak popped into my head as I sobbed in my mother's arms.

Deep down, I knew I had to be strong for my family, but I wasn't sure if I was capable. I can't begin to explain the roller coaster of emotions. I was so proud of my accomplishment but so utterly deflated looking at myself. It was a constant struggle. It was something that you would have to personally experience to understand. I know people have had experiences like this, and I feel for them. I wouldn't wish it on anybody.

This was one of the few times I cried in front of a family member during my stay in the hospital. I was raised to be tough and eat my emotions for breakfast. But this was different. This was something I never expected or saw coming. This would take more strength than I had in me to overcome.

FLASHBACK

1994

In the spring of 1994, my parents split up. I don't have a solid memory of how it took place. All I remember was my mom was there one day, then gone the next. I now understand why they divorced, but at the time my brother nor I had any clues.

Our living arrangement was not traditional. Both parents agreed we would live with our dad throughout the school year, visiting our mother every other weekend. We would then spend the summer months with our mother.

After the divorce, my dad continued living in our home in Rayville, and our mom moved thirty minutes away to Monroe. To Jake and me, this made perfect sense. We would continue to go to school with all our friends, then go on a summer vacation every year to the big city of Monroe. Monroe was only about 55,000 people in 1994. Still, to a young boy, this seemed massive compared to Rayville, where only about 4,500 people lived. Two Christmases were pretty sweet too!

The childhood that I remember was satisfying. We never went to bed hungry; we had endless toys and friends to play with, and we were put to bed by our mom or dad almost every night.

Our dad was a little stricter than our mom. So, my brother and I really cut loose during the summer months. It never crossed our minds what a struggle this was for them, but they did the absolute best they could to meet our physical and emotional needs. Thank God that has never stopped, especially through all of this.

Because my mom had to work, we spent much of the summer with our Grandma Jerri. Grandma was Mom's mom, and she kept us busy with countless activities.

One summer, McDonald's was running their famous Monopoly prize game. Grandma took Jake and me to McDonald's every day for breakfast and lunch. If you have ever seen the documentary Super-Size Me, I want to be clear, he was not the first to try this experiment. At the time, no one was aware of the health concerns of eating McDonald's twice a day, every day, for three months. To us, Grandma Jerri was the coolest grandma in the world.

Sports have always been a huge part of my life. I played baseball, football, basketball, and golf. My favorite to least favorite is in that exact order. Baseball was my favorite because that's the sport I was best at. I was a pitcher, and I was good. I seemed to have the right mental attitude that a pitcher requires. No matter how tough of a day I was having, I never let things bother me to the point that I would become rattled. I just kept tossing that ball over the plate.

At the time to me, that's just how I was. But looking back, I believe my parents' divorce played a part in creating my unshakeable attitude. But God tends to find a way to use all things for good. No one could have possibly known this attitude would one day help me overcome the unthinkable.

CHAPTER 15
No More Skipping Reps

Soon I grew tired of staying on the main floor and began to look forward to my departure from the hospital to an inpatient rehab facility. But my white blood cell count was still too high for me to be released. One day I woke up, and sharp pains were coursing through my residual limb. I thought, "Oh no, here we go again." I was concerned that something significant was wrong and that I would have another surgery. Dr. Hoppe was also concerned. This pain was not as bad as the pain I had with the hematoma, but we knew something was off.

I went for a CT scan that revealed a fluid buildup in my residual limb. I had three drains attached to my limb that were supposed to drain the excess fluid while my wound healed. These drains were not getting all of it, so Dr. Hoppe thought I might need to have another one put in. This was horrible news to me. These drains were the size of a light bulb with a long clear tube inserted into my stump. A single stitch held the tube in place so it would not pull out of my skin. The tubes would get caught on my bedding, and the stitch would rip my skin. This was not a pleasant feeling, and it happened often. Now they wanted to add another drain, increasing the frequency of my skin being tortured.

My surgery was scheduled, now we just had to keep our fingers crossed that this would do the trick. This was considered minor surgery, and I would not have to be put to sleep. They would dose me and numb up my residual limb to insert a needle to find the fluid. Once the fluid source was found, they would insert a hose and stitch it down. The procedure was a success, and I now had four annoying drains to deal with.

My white blood cell counts improved, and I was given the green light to leave the hospital. My family and I decided to go to Methodist Rehab directly next door. This rehab facility was highly rated, and I would be close to my surgeons if an emergency came up. I would spend two weeks at Methodist.

During that time, I would go through daily rehab activities. I had to complete three hours of rehab each day. This was way more than I was used to at the time, but I had been through worse. And I had better not skip out on any of these like I sometimes did with football. This was not a game anymore.

When I first arrived at Methodist, they weighed me in. I was a mega heavyweight before being shot. The last weight I remembered was 280 pounds, and I was excited to see what my new weight class would be. The nurse punched buttons and wrote the number down.

"How much?" I asked.

She said, "200 pounds."

"Wow!" I thought. I hadn't weighed 200 pounds since I was in the eighth grade. Of course, I realized I was now missing a leg, but I still had lost close to thirty-five pounds, not counting my leg. Since I arrived late that afternoon, I wouldn't start rehab until the next day.

My room at Methodist was the nicest I had been in so far, spacious with wood grain trimmed furniture. On the sixth floor, I had a grand view overlooking the hospital complex. I laid in bed that night watching TV, excited about the upcoming day.

The nurse woke me up when she brought breakfast the following day. I looked down at the plate and was shocked at what I saw. Biscuits, bacon, eggs, milk, and coffee! The food at Methodist was far better than the food in the hospital.

I scarfed down breakfast and went ahead to get dressed. By going to Methodist, I had graduated from hospital gowns to my own personal wardrobe. I soon realized there is a reason sick patients wear hospital gowns. Putting on my shorts and T-shirt was a monumental task. It took me every bit of fifteen minutes to get all my clothes just right. The four drains stitched to my skin were the biggest obstacle to overcome.

First up was occupational therapy. The goal was to reteach me how to do the essential tasks. I mainly focused on navigating the bathroom, hygiene, getting dressed, sitting, and standing. I had to complete an assessment before we could get started. I passed with flying colors. I committed to working extremely hard in rehab to learn and do as much as possible.

Next came physical therapy. They did an assessment to gauge my level of mobility. I was asked to stand up out of my wheelchair, transfer to a walker, and navigate a few obstacles laid out on the floor. To me, this was baby stuff. I had been doing this for days in the hospital. "When are we going to get to the good stuff?"

They were impressed with how mobile I was on day one. We then sat down, and they asked me what I wanted to accomplish while at Methodist. I had been thinking about what I would need to master to get back to everyday life. I said, "I work outside, and a walker is not going to cut it. I need to be using crutches before I leave."

They said, "Okay, we can work on that. But crutches are much less stable. If you fall, you could injure yourself."

In my mind, I said, "Bring it on; I'm not scared." I told them I understood, but that's what I had my mind set on. Then I wheeled myself back to my room and waited for my new doctors to come by and check on me.

Methodist runs a lot like a hospital, even though it's not a hospital, but they have a lot of the same equipment and staff. I had two new doctors that would oversee my medication. Long gone were the days of my beloved Dilaudid IV drip. I was now taking pills, 10 mg of OxyContin twice a day and 10 mg of hydrocodone every four hours as needed. I had a handful of other medications, but these were the ones my doctors were concerned about.

I was physically addicted to opioids, and the doctors and I both were aware. I would not have survived the intense pain without them. They suggested that I keep taking the OxyContin but maybe hold off on the hydrocodone unless I was in severe pain.

On my first day of complete rehab, I woke up and skipped my hydrocodone dose. I called for my nurse to bring me the pill about midway through my workout. I felt horrible, and my body ached all over. Within ten minutes of taking the pill, I felt relief. This would be much harder than I thought. Over the next couple of days, I tried my hardest to skip hydrocodone doses. Each time I would, my body would scream out in pain.

I was getting stronger, but my infrequent opioid dose left me irritable and depressed. The littlest thing would set me off, and I would lash out at my nurses. Some of them most likely thought I was a jackass, but they were probably used to that from patients they knew experiencing withdrawals.

Not only was my mood altered, but my bowel movements were a complete mess. I would go from constipated to free-flowing liquid on a whim. I still had not graduated to using an actual toilet. The bedpan was my preferred method. I had finally built up enough strength where I didn't need assistance getting it under me, but I still needed someone to clean me up afterward. On occasion, I would be left lying on a pile of my own feces for twenty to thirty minutes at a time. This would all happen in the bed that I had to sleep in every night.

Sometimes I would become so mad that I would cry out and curse God for doing this to me. I blamed him for putting me in this position, even though it was really my fault. But it was easier to blame God, so that's what I went with most nights. My darkest nights in memory were while I was at Methodist. I now realize this was primarily due to the demon I was facing, opioid addiction, a demon that is not to be played with.

Dr. Hoppe had scheduled an appointment for me, so he could see how my wound was healing. I was excited to see Dr. Hoppe. We had become friends; he had visited me every day while I was in the hospital, and I hadn't seen him since being moved to Methodist.

A transport nurse came to wheel me across campus to my appointment. I told her that I wanted to try and wheel myself to the appointment. She allowed this but still walked beside me in case I needed help. My appointment was a long way away from my room. I did my best to wheel myself, but I could push no further at the halfway point. The transport nurse took the reins and finished the long trek.

Dr. Hoppe had a big smile on his face when he saw me. He asked how I had been doing and how I felt. Then he got down to business and started to check on my wound. He liked what he saw and started to ask me about the drains. I told him they were a major pain in the butt and went over in detail how much fluid each one was producing.

He said, "If one starts to fall below 15 ml a day, we can probably take it out." I beamed with joy and showed him the one producing less than that amount.

He said, "Okay," and started the process of removing it.

Man, I was pumped! One down, and three to go! Things were looking up! We said our goodbyes, and he told me same time next week. I wheeled myself back out to the waiting area to tell my transport nurse I was finished.

When I got to the waiting area, my nurse was nowhere in sight. I wheeled circles around the chairs, looking for her, but she had vanished. So, I decided to make the long trip across campus myself. I would have to wheel through this hospital wing, open up two doors, go down a hall, onto an elevator, up two floors, wheel across a long skywalk that had a slight up and downhill slope, navigate through tight hallways that twisted and turned like an Indy car track, go through a big set of double doors, pass the McDonald's and gift shop, go through the Methodist double doors, onto the elevator, and then go down the hall to my room.

"Piece of cake," I said to myself. The distance was probably a half-mile in total.

The first part of my journey was a breeze. But once I reached the skywalk, the bear jumped on my back. The first part was slightly uphill, and I was struggling. Then I lost control on the downhill side, and like a runaway train, away I went. I managed to slow myself just enough to not crash into the wall. Then on to the treacherous zigzag hallway.

Sporting bloodshot eyes and messy rag-washed hair, I wheeled past hospital staff in the hall with a crazed look on my face. They would slow down and look around for my supervisor when they saw me. None of them ever said anything, but they most likely thought I was a insane patient attempting a grand escape. As far as I know, security was never alerted of a runaway one-legged patient. I got through the hall and wheeled past the McDonald's.

"Man, I would kill for a box of those fries and a milkshake right now," I thought. But there was no time for that. I was on the adventure of a lifetime. I couldn't get distracted now. I went past the gift shop, through the double doors, onto the elevator, and up to the sixth floor.

I was breathing heavily when I passed the nurse's station. They looked up from their computer screens and squinted their eyes.

"Where did you come from?" one asked.

"My doctor's appointment," I said.

"Where's your transport?" the other asked.

"Beats me," I said.

They looked at each other and started whispering, I was building quite the bad boy reputation among the nurses. As you can imagine, I was beaming with pride over this accomplishment.

My bad boy reputation would become solidified once I started hitting the weights. Methodist consisted of mostly older patients. I was one of the few young'uns. I would wheel myself over to the machine and poke the pin through the heaviest weight possible. My PT thought I was crazy, but she didn't know that I had an inner voice that was crazier than me. Coach Moffitt was back, and he was pushing me harder than ever. None of this was new to me. I had been here before. I just had to dig deep to pull it all back out.

"Nobody's gonna die out here" rang through my head and heart.

FLASHBACK

2008

Coach Moffitt sent all the incoming freshmen his bible for weight training, conditioning, and diet. I read through this book many times and did my best to follow the workouts. There were tough workouts in the book. One was fingertip push-ups. I tried hard to get good at them, but it seemed like I never made any progress, so I focused my time on running. I would run lap after lap around the track, getting ready for the dreaded 110 test. I trained for them by running the straights and walking the curves around the track. I think I got up to fifteen laps at one point, which equaled thirty 110-yard sprints.

Coach Moffitt would call to check in on me from time to time, and I would tell him how I was doing. He would give me nutrition tips to gain weight. One tip he gave me that I thought was strange was to eat cottage cheese every night before I went to bed. He explained how it was high in protein, and the content of cottage cheese took the body a long time to break down so it would fuel my body's muscle growth through the night. After we got off the phone, I ran straight to the store and bought cartons of cottage cheese.

When I explained to him what kind of running I was doing, I remember he sounded impressed, and he told me that I would have no problem with the conditioning test. I felt excited when he told me this. There was just something about how Moffitt spoke that would make you listen and pay attention. I am fortunate that I got the opportunity to listen to him for five years.

My freshmen year, the 110-test consisted of twenty-six 110-yard sprints. To pass, you had to run sixteen of them under the allotted time for your position. My freshman year, I was listed as a tight end, so my time was seventeen seconds. You would get forty-five seconds of rest between each sprint before you had to place your hand on the line and go again. If you ran sixteen sprints under your time, you would pass the test.

The night before summer workouts started, the team gathered for a meeting. I walked into the room and was in awe of all the great players. I had cheered these guys on during the 2007 championship season, and here I was sitting alongside them, preparing for the 2008 season. It was a surreal feeling, and the magnitude of my situation became real at that moment.

Coach Moffitt stood up to address the team and give the freshman orders for his summer workout program. He screamed, "I don't care if you get hit by a bus! You better drag your bloody ass in that weight room by 6 a.m.!" The older guys chuckled a little at Moffitt's intensity. Nobody in the freshman class dared to crack a smile.

The thick June air made my stomach turn the next morning. I was far too nervous to sleep the night before. Even though I had been training for this very day, doubt crept in on me. That day first on the to-do list was a heavy bench, squat, and clean to see where we stood strength-wise. Lifting heavy weights was never my strong suit. The other guys in my group out lifted me, and I really started to doubt what I had done training-wise.

"Maybe I'm not ready for these 110s," I thought.

Once they gauged everybody's strength, they sent all the freshmen off to class. There were a lot of firsts in those twenty-four hours; first team meeting, first-team workout, first college class, and first 110 conditioning test. It was sink or swim, and I felt like I had rocks tied to my feet that day.

Once I got to class, a nervousness built up inside of me. The older players were allowed to run the 110-test in the morning, and a few of them sat in class with me. They didn't say much, but the looks on their faces told me everything I needed to know. I thought there was a real chance I might die that afternoon while running.

After lunch, it all became real. None of my teammates looked confident. We had been told horror stories from the upperclassmen about the morning test, and I secretly hoped Moffitt would become ill, or lighting would strike and set fire to Football Ops. It soon became apparent that neither of these things would happen, and I had to face reality.

As I took the field to warm up, Moffitt appeared from his office, grinning from ear to ear. He ran out into the indoor facility skipping like a kid running to open Christmas presents and roaring like a diesel engine. All the stories were true. I no longer had any doubt whether Moffitt was a crazed madman.

We finished stretching, and he yelled for us all to run into the end zone. As he gave instructions on passing the test, several dozen of the upperclassmen walked out of the weight room and lined up along the sideline. They were all pointing, laughing, and placing bets on who would pass and fail. Moffitt barked the order for everybody to take their position behind the line.

The whistle blew, and I burst out of my stance, sprinting for the opposite end zone. Adrenaline took over, and I finished that first 110 well under my required time. Most of the guys did the same thing, and Moffitt warned us to calm down and find a steady pace. It took a couple of more reps to cross the line just under my required time.

On the eighth 110, I wanted to quit. Several guys had already failed the test, and I felt like I could be next. On rep ten, I could no longer breathe, and Moffitt started encouraging everybody to dig deep. "You are now entering another world! But it's okay, nobody's gonna die out here today!" he screamed. I wasn't so sure about that. My heart was beating so fast I felt I could croak at any second.

On the fourteenth sprint, I had reached my perceived physical limitations. My legs felt like jelly, and I had trouble standing upright. When I put my trembling hand on the line to wait on the whistle, something came alive inside of me. I burst from the line and felt a new rush of energy come over me. People call this a second wind, but this was more powerful than my first wind. I let out a roar and coasted through the line. I no longer felt tired. I could have touched the line, turned around, and ran back across the field under my time. When I finally realized I would pass the test, I felt a surge of confidence. I felt I belonged on that football team, and all my hard work had paid off.

I ran twenty-four 110s under my allotted time in my first year, and I felt like I was on top of the world for a day or two. But just because we passed the conditioning test didn't mean we got to coast for the remainder of the summer. Moffitt would continue to push us to the edge every day. This was when I came to grips with the amount of work it takes to achieve a goal.

CHAPTER 16
Wrestling

One sunny day I was at the weight machine when suddenly a helicopter dropped from the clear blue sky and landed on the roof of the hospital. The Medicopter had brought a patient in for surgery. I thought, "That's exactly how I arrived here. Man, I paid $20,000 for that helicopter ride, and I don't even remember it or got a selfie." I felt cheated.

Finally, I was ready to start using crutches. My PT had to search high and low to find a pair long enough to fit me. She found a beat-up, rusty set that had fallen on hard times. I didn't care what the crutches looked like. I would master this; my life depended on it.

Each day I would crutch down the hall; they would add up the distance I had traveled with a measuring wheel. I was always determined to travel farther than the day before. Day after day, my crutching improved, and I started to cover a long distance. The most impressive thing was that I never fell. I had a few close calls, but close doesn't count.

Although my strength kept improving, my mental state mainly stayed the same. I was still battling the demon called opioid addiction, and I felt as if I was losing. By the second week, I managed to stop taking my hydrocodone, but I was still popping OxyContin twice a day.

I mean, I'm not that tough.

My mental state was in shambles. I would cry myself to sleep most nights, confused about why I had been put through this. Not only did I feel sorry for myself, but also for my family. Their lives would also be forever changed because of this. I wondered if my son would grow to hate me since the number of things I would no longer be able to do with him was endless, and I began to believe he would resent me for it.

The big things in life were not on my mind. It was the little things; playing catch in the backyard, teaching him to ride a bike, and going on little adventures through the forest. I didn't see how any of that would be possible for me.

While I was in the hospital, Randy Light contacted my dad. Randy had adopted a son from India named Evan. When Evan was a baby, he was in a car crash that resulted in him losing both of his feet. His mother was also killed in the crash. Evan's family could not help him in the way he needed. Randy and his wife Jennifer heard this story and decided to adopt Evan. Evan grew up in the Light home and was now enrolled in LSU and working for the football team.

Because I played football at LSU, Randy heard my story and graciously offered to help inform us about the process of having prosthetics built. Evan had been wearing prosthetics nearly all his life, and they had vast knowledge of the process. Randy suggested that we get in touch with a practitioner named David Rotter. David lived and worked just outside of Chicago, Illinois. Randy told us that he had experience dealing with my level of amputation and generously offered to fly him to Jackson, Mississippi, to meet me. My dad accepted, and the flight was booked.

The first time I saw David, he gave me a mad scientist vibe. He was tall with dark hair and a salt-and-pepper scruffy beard. He gave me an empathetic look through his black-framed glasses and stretched out his hand to introduce himself. David got straight to business. He asked me if he could inspect my residual limb to see what I had for him to work with. We then went back into a conference room on my floor to talk things over. He was very clear from the beginning that this would not be easy. He explained all the challenges in detail and gave me an outline of what I needed to do so he could help me. He stressed the importance of staying lean and building up a strong core. He then showed us pictures and videos of patients he was currently working with. I had spoken with other practitioners who gave me similar advice, but none of them had David's confidence.

We were blown away by David's number of patients. He told me he was currently collaborating with a guy about my age who was six months ahead of me. He offered to have him reach out to talk me through the process from a patient's perspective. I agreed, and we continued our conversation.

After a couple of hours, it was time for David to catch his flight back to Chicago, and he left me with a bit of advice that took me back in time over a decade earlier.

My first year at LSU, my bench press was one of the weakest on the team. Coach Moffitt pulled me aside one day and suggested I do push-ups every night to improve. I gave him a nod, said, "Okay, Coach, sounds good," and then jogged back to my workout station. I did not ever do a single push-up before I went to bed, and my bench press suffered for my entire career.

I wasn't about to make the same mistake twice in my life. I would take David's advice seriously and do everything in my power to stay lean and build a strong core.

The nurse came into my room and told me I would take a shower that night. To this point, I only had sponge baths and was in serious need of a cleaning. I had built up an impressive funk; I knew this because most people avoided getting too close. Taking a shower turned out to be quite the job. My room was equipped with a roll-in shower and shower chair.

The process went like this: First, I would strip down naked in my bed. Then the nurse would tape a plastic bag over my drains so they wouldn't get wet. I would then transfer to the rolling shower chair, and she would wheel me into the shower.

This sounds easy as I write it out, but it was dreadful. The nurse must have pulled the stitches on my drains a dozen times, trying to tape the bag down. I would suck air through my clenched teeth each time, making a sizzling sound. This was my way of telling her she was doing a horrible job without being rude. After I sizzled no less than a dozen times, I slid out of bed onto the shower chair. The chair was almost too big to squeeze through the bathroom door. She had to sort of maneuver me at an angle to get the chair through. With one strong heave, she pushed me past the door, banging my knee on the wall in the process. "Sorry about that," she said. I didn't respond. She turned the shower knobs, giving me a bone-chilling shock.

"TOO COLD!" I screamed. She quickly adjusted the knobs until the water was just right. She then handed me a washcloth and left the bathroom.

I felt utterly helpless at that moment. I hung my head and looked over my pathetic excuse of a body. This was it; this was my life now, I thought. Never in a million years had I considered this to be an outcome. Suddenly I was brought from my sorrow with a violent urge to poop.

"I gotta poop!" I screamed out at the nurse.

She said, "It's okay, I'll clean it up later."

I hung my head in shame as poop splattered all over the shower floor. At that moment, I reached my lowest point. Tears burst from my eyes, and I wished I would have never survived. "How could you let this happen to me, God? Do you just enjoy torturing me?" I bawled like a baby for a couple of minutes, then looked around the bathroom for a quick way to end my misery.

I never had serious thoughts of suicide through all this. My thoughts were more around wishing I would have just died on the farm.

I finished my shower and called for the nurse to get me. Since the poop was more of a liquid than a solid, most had gone down the drain. She squeezed me through the door, once again banging my knee in the process. Now we had to remove the plastic bag. She carefully tried to peel the tape back while doing her best to avoid pulling a drain. I only sizzled at her a couple of times, so her second attempt was much improved. She handed me my clothes, and I transferred to my bed to get dressed.

As I put on my clothes, the nurse went into the bathroom to clean up my mess. After she finished, she came to my side and asked me if I needed anything else. I shook my head, no, and she turned and left my room.

"Okay," I thought, "now I just need to calm down and relax a little." I picked up the remote to see if there was anything good on TV. I found a basketball game to satisfy my interest and started to push the button to recline my bed.

Unexpectedly I felt a wet sensation on my left side. I jerked the covers back and saw that I was sitting on one of my drains. The top had popped off and leaked my disgusting bodily fluid all over the freshly cleaned bed and me. I reared back and threw the remote hard as I could, but it was on a stretchy cord. It ricocheted back and hit me in the shoulder. Tears erupted from my eyes. I cried and screamed and cursed God again, hoping I would get my point across to him this time. I mean, enough is enough, right? How much can one man take? I ignored the mess and closed my eyes. How could this day get any worse?

Everyone kept telling me God would not give me more than I can handle. Well, at that point, I didn't think God knew me very well. I did not know one person willing to switch places with me. If God loved me so much, why would he let this horrible thing happen to my family and me? I was not a bad person. I was just a regular guy minding my own business trying to scratch out a living to raise a family. "Why me?" That was the question I would ask God repeatedly, and I never got an answer.

Like Jacob, I wrestled with God. Perhaps also like Jacob, this was all part of the plan. After all, what happens when we wrestle? We come in close contact with whoever we are wrestling with.

As I neared the end of my second week at Methodist. I was getting around pretty well on my crutches. I was now traveling over 1000 feet at a time. I was supposed to go home in a couple of days, and I still had much to learn.

At Methodist, each patient would go through counseling sessions with a psychologist. I had two counseling sessions during my stay. In those sessions, I was taught breathing techniques, which I still use to relieve anxiety. I also discussed my thoughts about my predicament, and I was given valid suggestions and coping mechanisms.

In my second session, I brought up how I was concerned for my son, and he deserved a better dad than me. In my head, I went over my list of all things I had lost and began to spiral down my destructive thought pattern. In my eyes, my son deserved nothing but the best. How would I be able to give him that? I could barely get out of bed. I could not see the future I had always imagined us having. This new reality felt dark, depressing, and severely limited. I expounded on this for a couple of minutes, then waited for her reply. The following sentence from her mouth lifted me from that poisonous thought pattern.

She said, "I understand, but don't you think it's better that your son has a dad than not have a dad at all?"

At that moment, those words pierced my heart. She was right. How could I be so upset about my life when I came so close to not having a life at all?

I couldn't help but continue to ask why me. So many days and nights I spent tussling with the question of why. Every ounce of me wanted to believe there was a vital purpose for my hardship. Reality often reminded me that this thought was most likely a fantasy, a wish that would never come true. This was all a random act of bad luck followed by more bad luck that I must live life this way.

"God, are you up there? Are you listening? If so, I would really like to know the meaning of all this. I would love to know if there is a plan so maybe I can sleep tonight. Do you enjoy watching me suffer? Or do you not even care? How much longer do I have to put up with this?"

Most people who go through struggles get to look forward to a day when life will become normal again, but I don't have this luxury. No matter what happens from this point forward, I will never walk with grace and ease for the rest of my life. My leg will never grow back. No matter what happens, my life will be a constant physical and mental struggle from now on. This is the reality that I wake up to every morning.

CHAPTER 17
Purpose in Pain

It wasn't until I began to remember the mess my life was in before the accident that I began to scratch at a purpose behind this. I had gone so far astray, and I was no longer willing to make any attempt to change. I had everybody fooled on the outside. I looked and played the part of a successful twenty-nine-year-old with a beautiful family to perfection. On the inside, I felt lost and searched for reassurance that this was how my life was supposed to turn out. I would think back to my past mistakes and become angry at myself for letting my life turn out this way.

I felt like it was me against the world, and I had to control every aspect of my life. I felt overwhelmed by the expectations I had placed on myself and longed for a quick fix to stop the pain. I turned to alcohol, drugs, selfish behavior, and material things for answers. I felt like I needed these things to become the person I longed to be. It turns out I wasn't wrong about needing something to make me the man I was supposed to be. I was just wrong about what I needed.

How can a life ever be transformed without pain and suffering? This seems like a brutal way to accomplish something, but deep down, I think this is the only way I could start to understand. I had to encounter something that I did not have the strength to bear alone, and that is precisely what I have been given.

I now believe God has shown me a higher more noble purpose through the mistakes I have made. A purpose not centered around myself and how I can live the most comfortable life possible. It is a purpose to share my struggles, pain, and mistakes with others, so they know they are not alone. A purpose that boasts redemption and grace and that it is never too late to align with the spirit which calls to us from the light.

However, it will not come easy. It takes attention and participation to induce rebirth into new life. God is the light. He is the good which called to me at my lowest point and helped me start to picture how I could transform my life. I chose to go on an adventure walking toward the light, and I have faith it will lead me closer to God.

We are not only loved for our abilities but we are also loved because of our disabilities. In fact, it is through our disabilities that the light is brightest.

As I started to think about my life in this way, a new feeling arose. My challenges and circumstance would never change, but I began to feel deep inside my heart that good could come from this. My suffering would not be wasted. This feeling was enough to let me know I was on the right track.

I have begun to rediscover God's Word, and doors have started opening, those I never even knew existed that led to places I believed I would never be a part of, doors that have allowed me to share my story with millions of people and try to make the world a better place.

God has the means to rebuild someone's broken life back better than it was before. The catch is we must humble ourselves and understand that our ways of thinking are not always right. If we are open, honest, and noble in our pursuits, the answers and purpose will have a way of finding us.

All this time, I had been dwelling on what I had lost versus what I still had. I still had my life, my family, my house, my job, my friends, and my mind. I was lucky to have the opportunity to live and see what the tides of tomorrow might bring.

The next day would be my last at Methodist, and it was time for the ultimate test. I would crutch over 2000 feet and go up and down a flight of stairs. I woke up, ate breakfast, and had one thing on my mind, home. Part of me was happy, but another part was nervous. I was glad I would get home and see Liana and Barrett every day. I had only seen Barrett three times while in the hospital and rehab.

There was a soft knock at my door, and it was time for my final test. I started crutching right there in my room. I went down the hall to the elevator and down to the bottom floor. I left the elevator went through a botanical garden with a slight uphill slope, turned around, and headed for a flight of stairs. I navigated the stairs with only a tiny wobble and headed back to the elevator, up to the sixth floor, and back down the hall to my room.

I had done it! Now I was ready for the real world.

CHAPTER 18
A Whole New World

Liana

By the time Matt made it to rehab, the hospital, injury, and medication had really taken a toll on him. I distinctly remember visiting Matt one day in rehab. He was outside on a large balcony, sitting in his wheelchair alone, staring off into space. If it had been a scene in a movie, you would have thought the next part of the plot was this guy rolling himself right off the balcony.

I didn't say a lot because I could tell it was a day when nothing I could say or do would fix this for him. He tried to avoid eye contact, but I could see in his eyes he was completely broken and lost. Because of his drains, I couldn't sit in his lap, so I walked behind his wheelchair and wrapped my arms around him. I wanted to show him I saw him. I saw the pain and struggle his heart was wrestling with. He let me in just enough to let his walls come down just a little and smile.

Visiting Matt during his rehab stay was emotionally heartbreaking. I was so thankful for his progress and that he was even alive to be here with me, but this was when our true, totally new reality started to sink in. I saw how difficult it was for him to get dressed or go to the bathroom. I saw how frustrating it was for someone so independent all his life to not only need to ask for help but to have to ask for help. I knew he hated every single second of me seeing him struggle. Although I had Matt physically, I honestly didn't know if I would ever have Matt back emotionally. This broke my heart too.

On our fourth wedding anniversary, Matt was still in rehab. I thought we would try to make the best of it, so I planned to pick us up a nice steak dinner and sparkling champagne to celebrate, but Matt was in no mood for celebrating that day. As soon as I entered the room, I knew it had been a tough day, and it would be a tough night. He would hardly speak and stared straight ahead at the TV. My feelings were hurt, but I played it off and knew he needed some space. So, I casually told him I'd go pick up dinner and be back in an hour. I cried the whole car ride to the restaurant and the entire car ride back to the hospital. I picked up wine instead of sparkling champagne because I would need it. I was a wreck. It wasn't tears of sadness this time, though. This time I cried because I had begun to feel like him. I was angry.

What had we ever done so wrong in our lives to deserve this? Was this how every day would be for us? Would Matt be angry forever, and rightfully so? Was I strong enough to manage this? I poured the wine into a Styrofoam cup so I could sneak it into his room, wiped my tears, and was determined to salvage the night. When I returned, Matt wanted to eat in silence and even tried to tell me I should probably just drive back home instead of staying there with him. The nerve! I regretted not bringing the whole bottle of wine in.

I learned a valuable lesson that night.

I could wear my feelings on my sleeve as much as I wanted and could throw myself a pity party as often as necessary. The problem was, what good was that for Matt and my marriage? Matt was internally dealing with something of which I could never begin to understand the true magnitude. I didn't lose my leg. As much as I tried to relate and thought I understood what he was going through, that was totally different from being the one disabled. I thought it was about me too, at the time, which, in some ways, it was. I didn't need to be his punching bag through this, but I needed to be prepared. I would have to be strong enough to take hits without letting them hurt my feelings or cause us to take steps backward in our marriage.

It is better to suffer than to cause suffering.

We couldn't afford even the slightest step back. Too much was at stake. My expectations and role in our marriage needed to adapt to our new circumstances. As much as my heart wanted everything to be okay and longed to make all the bad disappear, I couldn't expect Matt to pick up the pieces as if nothing had happened. Matt had so much to process at the time. It was just as much my responsibility to our marriage as his to make the best of our new situation and not let it ruin us. Sounds easy, right? It certainly wasn't. Our first year after the accident was full of ups and downs.

We chose to fight for each other and not against each other, and it truly made a difference.

On Matt's discharge day, I was a nervous wreck. At the same time, I was beyond excited. This would be huge for us. I spent the weeks before preparing our home to be handicap accessible, which was a whole new world for me. Observing him in the rehab setting allowed me to see what kind of day-to-day obstacles he would face. I researched and got advice on making our bathroom safe for Matt. I rearranged our furniture to make broad and open walkways in our rather tight space. I also tried to develop a reasonable but fair toy solution for Barrett. All I could see were tripping hazards everywhere, but this was our life. I'm a big planner, and as much as I wanted everything to be prepared for Matt when he came home, I knew I couldn't prevent every obstacle.

I arrived at Methodist prepared to help pack everything up and couldn't believe what I saw when I entered Matt's room. He had loaded up all his belongings on a rolling cart by himself, waiting by the door to be picked up. He wasted no time. As soon as I entered the room, he signed discharge papers, and we headed down the elevator. He was ready to go!

I smiled the whole way home.

Imagine not spending time with your husband outside of a hospital room for almost sixty days. Having him choose the radio station and pick where we would grab lunch was the best feeling for me. After going through a traumatic event like this, even the smallest of everyday normalities were greatly appreciated.

All three of us being home together for the first time since the accident was surreal. Matt's entire mood seemed to lift. He seemed so peaceful and thankful to finally be home. Deep down, I was still scared that he was hiding dark thoughts.

Each morning before I left Matt to drive to work, I would study his face and try to read him. On my drive to school, I would replay his facial expression repeatedly and pray that he was mentally okay and not thinking of ending his own life. So many people warned me of the signs of a person contemplating suicide, and I kept watch over my husband like a hawk.

I spent most evenings staring at him as if I hadn't seen him in years. I watched him hold and play with Barrett thinking I couldn't believe we had made it to this moment. It almost seemed like nothing had ever happened when, at the same time, everything had happened. Matt fought to survive the accident, and God allowed him to live. He surprised everyone with his progress in rehab. The real work of moving on with life began next.

CHAPTER 19
You Can't Do It Alone

Matt

The home was a little different than the way I had left it. While I was gone, countless friends and family pitched in to keep the yard tidy and assembled assistance devices to help me navigate the house. Liana's coworkers put together a meal train, so we didn't have to cook dinner for a month. All around me, people were more than willing to lend a helping hand. We received over $150,000 from GoFundMe and private gifts. I was blown away by the support I received from the community.

I would not be where I am today without these countless acts of kindness.

I used a walker to get around my house for the first month. It was complicated to get comfortable in bed. I spent most nights getting little sleep while tossing and turning in pain and agony. On my first night home, I had to get up in the middle of the night to use the bathroom. I'm positive I woke Liana up with the noise of me grunting and straining to get out of bed and my walker loudly clicking with each step across the room. I got to the bathroom and fumbled in the dark to find the light switch. I hobbled over to the sink and stared at myself in the mirror. I didn't recognize this man. This man had long scraggly hair and seemingly carried the weight of a lifetime of pain and suffering. This man looked beaten, broken, and tired. I stared at myself and fought back the tears.

Every dream I spent countless hours of how I would live out my life had disappeared in the blink of an eye. I didn't have the knowledge or energy to start planning my life again just yet.

I longed for the familiar, familiar sights, smells, and actions, but everything was different now, and I couldn't figure out how I would go on. Everything in my past was now erased, and I was forced to learn what could be recreated and how to go about doing it. The simple things now seemed complicated, and the complex things seemed impossible.

After I grew tired of my pity party and fighting to balance on one leg, I made a move to get back to bed. I had to shift my walker to the left a few inches to turn toward the door. I dropped my weight down onto the walker to move my foot into position. I put my weight back down on my foot and tried to pull the walker around in front of me. The walker's leg got stuck on the bathroom rug, and I lost my balance and began to fall. As I fell, instincts took over, and my body reacted as if my left leg was there to catch me. Obviously, this was a trick, and I landed firmly on the tile floor. My eyes grew wide from the adrenaline rush as I looked around the room in disbelief. This was the first time I had fallen after losing my leg. I landed on my residual limb and expected sharp pains to course through my body.

I handled the fall well. When I realized nothing was broken or out of place, my mind turned to how I would get up. I looked around the room and discovered my best option. I would need to drag myself across the bathroom to the bathtub to put my back against it and push myself up with my arms so I could stand. As I stood up, I looked back at my reflection in the mirror.

At that moment, I came to grips with the reality that I would fall, but I had the power to get back up again. I had to find a way to get back up, not just for me but for my family.

Liana had started back to work after her principal had generously allowed her to take over a month off to stay with me in Jackson. Doctors suggested that I not be alone for a couple of weeks for fear that I fall and injure myself. But what do doctors know anyway? I told Liana I would be fine by myself, and she was only minutes down the road if I needed her.

The silence in the house after she and Barrett left each morning was eerie. I had spent the last fifty-three days in the hospital and rehab, where there was a constant pitch. But not here. Except for the TV, there was dead silence. For a time, I sort of missed the energy of the hospital, but that wouldn't last long. I was free to do what I wanted and when I wanted; eat what I want and when I want and sleep as long as I want and when I want. It was good to get my freedom back, but I still had to stay focused on the mission, learning to walk again.

After consideration, we decided I would go to the Glenwood outpatient rehab. The clinic was not far from my house, and my insurance was accepted. Liana was supposed to take me in for my evaluation. As usual, she was dragging around the house, making us late. I am terrified of being late, thanks to none other than Tommy Moffitt.

FLASHBACK

August 2008

A week into fall camp, we were nearing the end of practice my freshman year. Coach Henson threw me into the three tight ends set with the ones just to see what I could do. This was my first time running a play with the first-team offense, and I didn't want to disappoint. When the ball was snapped, I fired off the line with everything I had. I locked up with the defensive tackle in front of me, and I stood my ground, to my surprise! It took every ounce of strength I had to keep the defensive lineman from pushing me backward, and I was impressed that I could stone one of our starting defensive linemen.

It was nearly the end of practice for his defense, and I mainly had watched the whole day while he had run more than sixty plays. It felt like an eternity that I had to lock up and keep him from advancing into the backfield. The running play was designed to go toward my side, so there would likely be a pileup because it was short yardage.

As I was locked up with my guy, the defensive lineman to my inside slipped the offensive tackle. As he was trying to squeeze through the small gap, he lost his footing and landed on the heel of my right foot while it was planted firmly in the turf. Immediately it felt like my foot broke in half. I fell on my face and cringed at the pain. Luckily, I could get up and hobble off the field toward the training room. The good news was that my foot was not broken. However, I had severely strained some ligaments and would need to go through some therapy for a couple of days.

They ruled me out of the next couple of practices, and I spent them in the training room getting stem, ice, and walking on the underwater treadmill. I went in early one day to start on my therapy. This was a light day, and all we had was a maintain lift and walk-through that afternoon. I was walking on the underwater treadmill in the training room as everybody was getting ready for the workout. I finished my walk on the treadmill, and the trainers told me I needed to go lift. So, I got out of the water, went into the locker room, changed clothes, and hobbled down the long hall toward the weight room.

As I was rounding the corner, I could hear Coach Moffitt giving instructions. I busted through the door, and Moffitt was standing on a purple wooden storage box with the whole team surrounding him. He was looking up at the TV when he heard the door open. He whipped his head around and saw my goofy selfhobbling through the door. He immediately started yelling and cursing me because I was late for his workout. He told me to get out of his sight while thoroughly embarrassing me in front of the team. Not knowing where else to go, I went back into the training room to do more therapy. I told the training staff that Moffitt kicked me out of the weight room and cussed me pretty good.

Five minutes later, after a bag of ice was wrapped around my foot, Coach Moffitt kicked in the training room door, yelling my name at the top of his lungs, "Where is Matt Branch?"

I didn't have to say anything. I was sitting right there by the door when we made eye contact. I felt like the smallest human on earth. He yelled at me to get that fresh bag of ice off my half-broken foot and meet him on the indoor practice field. Then turned around, re-kicked in the swinging door, and stormed back to the weight room.

I unwrapped my foot at a snail's pace. When I looked up, the whole training staff was staring at me bug-eyed like this might be the last time they would see me alive.

I laced my shoe up and slowly hobbled to the indoor practice field. As I walked through the double doors, I noticed that the LSU cheerleaders were practicing in the endzone on the far side of the indoor field. Moffitt had not arrived yet, so I sat down on a bench behind the field goalpost and feared the worst. A couple of minutes later, Moffitt kicked through yet another door, somehow screaming even louder than he had in the training room, making for quite the scene.

His voice echoed around the indoor field as he threw brilliantly worded constructive insults at me. Moffitt always has a comedic touch with his words. Whoever was receiving the wrath wouldn't dare to laugh, but everyone else in earshot couldn't help but crack up. He screamed at me so loud that the cheerleaders on the opposite end of the field dropped their pom-poms and gawked in silence like they weren't sure if they should leave or not. He shouted at me for about thirty seconds, but it felt like thirty minutes. At the end, he said, "Alright, I know you can't run, so you will pencil roll."

Pencil rolls are where you lay flat on the ground and roll the field's length. This may not sound very tough, but after about fifty yards of rolling like a pencil, you become so dizzy and sick that you are guaranteed to puke. As I rolled across the field, I could hear the cheerleaders playfully giggling, and I was very embarrassed. The turf felt coarse and rigid, and tiny rubber pellets stuck to my arms and legs and got down in my underwear. This was genuinely miserable, and as expected, I threw my guts up after the first one hundred yards. Long story short, Moffitt had made his point, and I was never late to a workout for the rest of my career.

CHAPTER 20
Putting in the Work

The Glenwood clinic was a bit underwhelming. I was accustomed to the massive clinic of Methodist, where they had three different floors of equipment and a giant staff to go along. Glenwood Outpatient in Monroe was manned by one PT, and the clinic itself was about the size of my bedroom at home. But it had all the necessary equipment, and it was close to my house.

Lauren Branch was the PT who ran the clinic. You may be wondering if we are related, and to answer your question, no, we are not, same last name but no relation. Lauren is a highly skilled PT with years of experience. Her husband, Dr. Billy Branch, is my physician. I would visit him every few weeks to get prescriptions refilled and check on my progress. And no, this was not an elaborate plan to keep all my medical records confined to only one family of medical professionals. It just worked out this way.

I would go to Lauren's clinic three days a week for ten weeks straight. Each session was precisely one and a half hours. I obviously spent a ton of time at her clinic. To this day, she will probably tell you that she didn't do much for me; I did it all myself. But Lauren didn't know everything she was doing. Lauren created an environment that was inviting, warm, and friendly. I thrived in this environment, and I could talk with her about what I was going through. I spoke with her about why this happened a lot.

Lauren and I became friends over those ten weeks, and she helped me understand that people didn't see me differently just because I looked odd. Just because I had been through this horrible accident and amputation didn't mean I wasn't still the man I was meant to be.

I slowly started to gain my physical strength back. I was working hard every day at PT, and on my off days, I would do work at home. When I was in the hospital, one of my goals was to go turkey hunting that spring. As my strength grew, that goal became more of a reality. Liana thought I was kidding about turkey hunting, but I wasn't.

Texas turkey season was set to open on March 31st, so I called up my dad and planned a trip. We were about two weeks away from leaving, so I made it a point to practice the things I would have to do while hunting: sit and stand using only crutches, travel medium distances, and carry weight.

As the date neared, Liana voiced her concerns. She did not like me going hunting again, not one bit. In the back of her mind, I think she hoped I would give it up after nearly being killed while doing it. I explained that hunting was something I couldn't just give up. I had spent too much of my life doing it, and my passion for it would not simply turn off. We continued to talk about this for several days before she ultimately realized I was a lost cause, and hunting and the outdoors were too much of a part of who I am.

FLASHBACK: RAISED OUTDOORS

My passion for hunting started at a very young age. When I was in the fourth grade, my dad bought me a pellet gun for Christmas. We had a five-acre backyard throughout my childhood, and I didn't let it go to waste. My brother and I climbed trees and made countless forts and trails in the natural vegetation. This yard was paradise for a child with an imagination, and I have so many great memories of playing in it.

Every day after school, I would run inside, grab my pellet gun, and patrol the yard, searching for birds and squirrels. I pretended the birds and squirrels were big game animals. My dad most likely thought I had a problem, but I didn't care. Shortly after getting my pellet gun, I dropped it on the driveway, and all the sights fell off. I had to aim by looking down the barrel, and I missed often.

One day I tried to tape an old pair of binoculars to my pellet gun and draw crosshairs on the lens with a sharpie. To a ten-year-old, this seemed like a brilliant idea; let's just say the birds and squirrels were safe on my patrols. Growing up in a yard like this helped my passion for the outdoors blossom in my adolescent years.

CHAPTER 21
Lone Star State Bound

Days before we were scheduled to leave for Texas, I had an appointment with Dr. Branch. It was time to refill my prescriptions. As we talked in his office, he told me I needed to think about weaning myself off OxyContin. I was still taking two ten-milligram pills every day. I listened to his advice, grabbed my scripts, and left his office. When I got back in my truck, I decided that I was done taking pain meds. And from that day on, I have not taken another pain pill.

Looking back, this may have not been the best idea. There I was, two days away from going on a trip with my dad and youngest brother. What father and son duo don't tend to get on each other's nerves from time to time? Then throw on top of that the son detoxing from a severe opioid addiction. There is bound to be an explosive dynamic.

So, on March 30th, my dad, brother, and I set out west on a turkey hunting adventure. Here I was, the most experienced turkey hunter of the group, and I could barely get around. This was bound to be tons of fun!

It felt good to get back out on the ranch we had been hunting for the past four years. I had grown to love this little piece of heaven in the Texas hill country. The landscape was beautiful. A healthy mixture of live oak, mesquite, and cedar covered the ranch. It was a hunter's dream, with a well-managed deer herd, turkeys, and wild hogs. The camps were nestled near the bank of the San Saba River, which flowed through central Texas. They were also well made and maintained with all the comforts of home at arm's reach.

The Reata River Ranch owners are as good as gold. We had grown to become friends over the past few years. They were also very supportive of me in my time of need, and I will be forever thankful to them.

I quickly realized I had a long way to go in my recovery. It was a struggle navigating the tricky Texas landscape. Everything in Texas either sticks you or bites you, and it all was having a field day with my crippled ass. I pulled thorns out of my leg and backside for a month after that trip. But I was determined I wouldn't give up. I would keep hunting until it was time to go home.

I had no luck through the first two days. We heard many turkeys gobbling, but I just couldn't get close enough. It all came down to my last afternoon. My cousin who saved me convinced me I needed to drink a beer to change my luck, so I gave it a try. I hadn't touched a sip of alcohol in three months, and the beer didn't taste as good as I had remembered. I told my dad to drop me off in a spot we had heard birds gobbling the day before. He drove to the area, helped me get set up, and left. As I sat there, I started to replay all I had been through over the past three months.

To this day, I still have trouble believing that it all happened.

While sitting there, I had a strange feeling when I looked down at my gun. I had respected guns my entire life. I grew up around them and was comfortable using them. I never considered that I would mishandle one, and it would nearly cost me my life. Chills ran up my spine as the utter terror of being shot point-blank ran through my mind.

I have continued hunting, and to this day, I get a hollow feeling in my stomach when I'm around a gun I know is loaded. I don't guess that will ever go away.

When I think back to December 28th, the events that took place strike me as odd. This was the worst day of my life, and hopefully, it will never be topped. All the things that led up to the climax of my gun going off are hard for me to believe. Everything in me screams that this was no accident. There are simply too many strange events that happened that directly led to me being shot. The events affected where I was, where my gun was, and being exposed and loaded.

For all you hunters and gun enthusiasts, I want to be clear, I am not trying to make an excuse for myself. Believe me, I know this should have been prevented if I had taken that single shell back out of my gun. But let's say I would have taken that shell out. That does not change the fact that all these strange things happened. Even if I had not been shot, this would still go down as the most bizarre hunt I have ever had.

The gun strap broke, I went the wrong way, crashed the four-wheeler, broke my phone, wet gun case, made a bad shot, didn't get a shot, and the dog shot me.

Maybe you are like me, and tragedy has also come into your life. I once heard a statistic that ninety percent of people will face some sort of tragedy in their lifetime. If this number is indeed true, it seems to me that suffering is one of the most common things that we humans share.

No one desires to go through involuntary suffering. Most people will run from it at all costs. We all have a strong urge to purge it from our lives and overcome it. What is not always clear is how we do this.

I do not have the power to change my circumstance, but I cannot give my circumstance the power to change me for the worse.

Maybe this is why I chose to go hunting so soon after leaving the hospital. I knew I must confront the thing that scares me the most. This is how you move on. This is how you become brave and endure the suffering.

I cannot take credit for this wisdom. In the book of Numbers, the Israelites spent forty years experiencing many types of suffering in the desert. At one point, they were continuously bitten by serpents. This may be worse than getting shot. They begged and pleaded for their lives that the serpents would quit biting them.

Eventually, a solution was revealed. God told Moses to build a bronze statue of a serpent, place it on a pole, and lift it up for all to gaze upon. The Israelites had to face their fear. They had to confront their suffering to overcome it. Although facing the bronze snake did not stop the serpents from biting them, it did stop the poison from killing them. Psychologically speaking, the same thing goes for us today. If you want to overcome something, you must first face it.

Jesus Christ also points us to this strange story in John 3:14. He says that he should be lifted like the bronze snake. I can't help but wonder what exactly Jesus is trying to tell us here. Jesus on the cross has been the Western culture's symbol of suffering for over 2,000 years.

Jesus was young, innocent, betrayed by his friends, handed over to the mob, and crucified on the cross in front of his mother. He was lifted on that cross for all to gaze upon him. He told us that all who do look, who do believe, will have eternal life or a life that will be of value for all human existence, a life of service, sacrifice, and agape love, a virtuous life.

It is obvious through this tragedy that I have physically suffered. However, what is not obvious is spiritual suffering. The fact that I am the cause of this tragedy was and is humiliating. Often, I wonder how many people have heard my story, and their first reaction was, "What an idiot." To be clear, I agree. What an idiot.

One day I sat down and read through the comments on an online news article, and my suspicions were confirmed. Of the thousands of comments, the majority called me an idiot. I cannot lie, although I agree, it still hurt deeply. Even though the whole experience was humiliating, I still must gaze upon it and see if there is anything worth learning.

In Matthew 5:3, Jesus says, "Blessed are the poor in spirit for theirs is the kingdom of heaven" (NKJV).

In other words, blessed are those who have been humiliated or humbled enough to see the deceit of pride and prepare themselves to receive the highest of responsibilities.

To me, this verse is not only talking about the materially poor but the spiritually poor. Those who have betrayed themselves must now understand that they must look outside and above themselves to align with a new significance and higher value in life.

By no means does this exhaust all Christ has done. No matter if you believe the stories of Jesus to be metaphors or historical facts, you cannot deny the significance they have had on human civilization. Sometimes the best way to figure out where you are going is to better understand exactly where it is that you have come from.

So far, the afternoon had been uneventful. I hadn't seen any turkeys even though I had been calling every twenty or so minutes. Maybe it was because I'm terrible with a turkey call. Out of nowhere, to my left, I caught movement. I could just make out something moving through a mass of cedar. "It's a turkey!" I thought. And sure enough, it was. It was a lone hen pecking around in the grass twenty yards from me.

Then suddenly, out of the blue, she started calling. She let out a string of clucks and purrs, and I thought to myself, "thank you, God, for giving me a little help over here." Not five minutes later, two gobblers popped up in the direction the hen came from. This was my chance to make it happen. I slowly reached for my shotgun and patiently waited on them to clear the cedar thicket. After what felt like an eternity, the first gobbler popped his red and blue bald head out, then snapped it right back behind the cedar.

I could tell he knew something wasn't right. The second gobbler stepped past the cedar and out into the open out of curiosity. The warm afternoon sunlight enhanced the colors of his beautiful, fully flocked fan. In a way, it seemed he was looking back, calling the first gobbler a chicken for not walking out into the open. I raised the barrel of my Remington 870 shotgun until the bead was placed just at the base of his flabby neck and squeezed the trigger. The bird instantly fell dead, and I had done what I came here for. I could take this turkey home and enjoy it at the kitchen table with Liana and Barrett. Overall, our Texas turkey hunt was a success. But it was a success in more ways than one. It showed me how much further I had to go if I had any hope of living a life close to my old one.

CHAPTER 22
Fear of Failure

Liana was glad to see me when I got back home. I don't think she took a deep breath the whole time I was in Texas. I can't blame her. I told her all about my trip, the story of my successful hunt, and how difficult it was getting around the treacherous terrain.

Not long after I got back, David Rotter texted me to see how I was doing. I told him my wound was healing nicely and let him know I still hadn't decided where I would have my prosthetic made. I was also considering using somebody local for the convenience of it. Chicago is a twelve-hour drive from Monroe. What would I do if my leg broke or needed to be adjusted? I couldn't just hop in the car and drive up to Chicago out of the blue. After all, I still had a job and other responsibilities to consider.

Another couple of weeks went by, and David texted me again. This time he asked for pictures of my residual limb and sent me a video of Josh Stuber walking on his prosthetic. Josh is the guy my age who was about six months ahead of me in his recovery. Josh walks beautifully with a hip disarticulation prosthetic, and I consider him a friend and mentor. After seeing that video, I asked David if he had any dates available in May. He sent back what he had open, and I confirmed a two-week appointment.

Even though I had been working hard and regained a portion of my strength, I was still nervous. Every other practitioner and hip disarticulation amputee I had reached out to told me it would likely take me months, if not years, to learn to walk correctly. I listened to their advice, but I kept telling myself I was not like most other hip disarticulation amputees. I didn't know of any hip disarticulation amputees who had played college football and had natural athleticism like me. Even though I played guard, I was always athletic for a big guy.

I circled the dates on my calendar and prepared for my trip to Chicago. By this time, I had transitioned to forearm crutches. These crutches were not as stable as underarm crutches, but they were better suited for a lifetime crutch user. They required more strength and balance, but they allowed me a bigger range of movement.

It didn't take long for Barrett to refer to my crutches as another member of the family. He would sometimes sit and stare at them with burning curiosity, trying to decide what to make of them. Anytime he noticed them on the floor next to me, a childlike instinct came over him to grab one and run far away from me like a bandit making out of a jewelry store.

After months of this annoying behavior, he began reaching out and grabbing them as I would walk by, causing me to nearly fall no less than a half dozen times a day. My mischievous son gets all the credit for my crutching excellence.

At physical therapy, I started doing bodyweight dips. I got to where I could do thirty at each session. I could never do dips while at LSU, but there I was, cranking them out like I was born for it.

I could not fail at this; I had experienced heartbreaking failures in my life, and I did not want to revisit that dark place again.

FLASHBACK

January 2012

If you are an LSU football fan, you remember this date. Maybe not very fondly, but you remember. It's hard to forget, even now over ten years later. The LSU Tigers were playing in the BCS National Championship on college football's biggest stage. I imagine there has never been a youngster in America who picked up a football and hasn't dreamed of being here. We were just as ready for this game as every other game that season. When we loaded the charter buses, every player was mentally sharp and prepared for the task at hand. Everybody knew what was at stake, but we treated it like any other game.

As we walked into the Superdome on January 9, 2012, the familiar smell of cheap bourbon and corndogs lingered outside the stadium. The feeling of greatness in the air made the hairs on my neck stand and dance. This was our time. This was going to happen; we all felt it.

I'm about to disclose my experience and recollection of the events that took place during the 2012 national championship game. This game sticks out in every Tiger fan's mind as the most disappointing loss in recent memory. And I can speak for all the players on that team. We feel the same way.

Rumors circulated about fights in the locker room among players and coaches. Stories circulated of Coach Saban getting our practice footage in the Superdome—he had a well-earned reputation for winning at any cost—stories that Coach Miles had placed bets against us in Las Vegas. This is just part of the craziness that surrounds such a huge event, especially when it was a rematch between two SEC powerhouses.

We were 13–0, undefeated, ranked number one, and had beaten Alabama in a defensive heavyweight fight 9–6 in overtime in the regular season. A lot of folks, including me, didn't think Alabama should be there after not winning the conference or even making it to the conference championship. They were good, though. And their name, and the prestige of Coach Saban, got them a rematch.

It's hard to beat a team like that twice. So, things were crazy. Rumors of our QB being out late on the town late the night before the game were also swirling. There were more that we heard and more rumors on the street. I'm sure I'm missing several, but these are the ones I can remember ten years later. I do not have knowledge or proof of all the rumors above, but here's what I know.

Our entire game plan was based around 9, our quarterback, and his amazing skill set. The team knew we could win with this plan; we had already done it once that season. Well, Coach Saban being who he was, wrote up a dominant game plan to defend 9 and his skill set. Everybody in the football world knows that if Saban keyed on stopping something, he'd stop it. And you better have a plan B.

It was clear that our game plan would not work after the first couple of drives. Even the fans could see how clearly the Alabama defense was keying the run. I was stunned and thought we would change things quickly. But early on, our defense showed its dominance too. We were still in the game at halftime; it was only 9–0. We were just two big plays away from being on top with our weapons on offense. But it was apparent that the plays we were currently running had to stop, and we needed to pivot and give 12 a series to try and find a weakness in the Alabama defense. I want to be clear, this is no critique of 9. This is a recognition of the tremendous Coach Nick Saban is. He had us dead to rights, and he knew it.

At halftime, everybody expected energy and excitement from our coaches, but what we got was shocking. A typical halftime consisted of Coach Stud at the board, acting like he just took an espresso shot. He would ask every player on offense what they saw and explained what he saw from the press box. Coach Miles would stand at his side, listening and focused on every word, and agreeing or disagreeing with what was discussed. It was a sight to see, and every offensive player would be locked in and focused. But on this night, there was no sign of that structure.

Coach Stud was standing off to the side, not saying a word.

The players were looking at the coaches and around at each other confused and disoriented. We were wondering what the plan was. What were we going to do differently in the second half? But there was no communication whatsoever. Coach Miles seemed to be hiding in the corner like Coach Klein on The Waterboy, not wanting to speak with anyone but the football resting in his lap.

As a four-year player, I was shocked. Were we just going to give up right now? At the time, I thought the coaches just didn't have an answer for Alabama's defense, and the only way we would score was if 7 returned a kick or had a pick-six. But now that I have had the chance to talk to some other guys on the team, I think there was more going on than what meets the eye.

I think it's safe to say Coach Miles is a stubborn man. I listened to him talk and watched his actions for five years, and I don't have any problems saying that. Well, that night, I believe he reached a whole new level. I genuinely think that Coach Stud wanted to give 12 a series. I had even heard that he suggested this to Coach Miles over the headset during the game, and Coach Miles replied, "If you want to keep your job, you will shut the hell up and call the plays." What was a man supposed to do when his boss told him that? I have a job, and I know what I would do.

I also know that during the game, one of our team captains was urged by many of the LSU higher-ups to get on the headset and tell Coach Miles we had to try quick passes. They were stacking the box and playing the run hard, and we were never going to get anywhere. Coach Miles's reply was, "You need to shut the hell up and block better." How was a team expected to win when the head coach treated valid suggestions like that? I heard other accounts from players of similar conversations with Coach Miles that night. His response stayed consistent.

After a series, 12, who was wearing a headset, would take it off and start to throw a little to warm up. Each time I saw this, I had a spark of hope that we would at least try something new. By no means am I suggesting that we would have won that game if 12 had gone in. But at least we could look back and say we exhausted all options and did everything we could to win. But now, because of one man's stubbornness, thousands of fans, our players, everyone who bleeds purple, and gold have regrets and forever wonder what could have been of one of the greatest teams in LSU history.

I recall a play early in the fourth quarter where it was third, and four and 9 turned around and handed the ball off to 44. I was in utter disbelief when I saw this. 44 had hardly touched the ball and had not gained a single yard all year. He was a hell of a blocking FB, but a ball carrier? Not so much. It was still a two-score game, and this was the best play we could dial up when we were in decent field position. At this point, I lost all hope.

As lucky as Coach Miles had been throughout his career with the multiple clock mismanagements and the only coach to get a two-loss team to the national championship, there were no miracles here for him. The Mad Hatter didn't have enough luck to overcome a busted game plan and an utter lack of willingness to adapt. I knew that no matter what, he was not willing to take the advice of his staff and players, and we were going down in flames.

Our defense held its own and kept us in the game much longer than we should have been. But in the end, the offense let us all down. The offense only gained one first down in the first half and never crossed the fifty-yard line. We gained four first downs in the second half and crossed the fifty-yard line once. Pretty pathetic.

Look, Alabama was the better team that night, and no matter what we tried, we might have still lost. But I can't help but be pissed off at how we lost. If we had pulled out all the stops and gone down swinging, I could live with that. But that's not what happened. We cowered down and allowed stubbornness to be the cause of a lifetime of regrets.

I believe if Coach Miles could do it all over again, he would have done things differently. When we beat Alabama in the regular season, 12 was on a hot streak. We were blowing opponents out with him at the helm. But again, I give credit to Coach Saban. He wrote up a defensive game plan that shut 12 down. So, what did we do? We put 9 in the game and found a little success. We moved the ball enough to get within scoring range a couple of times and let our defense win the game for us. If it worked the first time, why would you not try it the second time?

To this day, I have not watched that game, and I believe this is true for many other players on the team. There were painful tears shed in the locker room that night. The seniors did not deserve to go down like that, and my heart went out to all those guys.

The next day the team scattered like ants after you disturbed their bed. Guys went off to pursue NFL stardom. The underclassmen went home to wipe their memory with hobbies and chemical substances. At that time in my life, I was more of a chemical substance guy, and we only had a handful of days off before the spring semester started.

Sometimes my memory fails me, but I recall that first team meeting a little off the wall. It was almost as if Coach Miles had no memory of the national championship game. I think he had wholly wiped that off his conscience. Looking back, that may not have been a bad strategy. The team was a little caught off guard, and instead of walking around heartbroken for days, we just moved on as best as we could all at once.

This was my final year to wear purple and gold. I often wish I could go back and warn my twenty-two-year-old self about what was just around the corner. On the outside, I put on a face that told everyone I would work hard and prepare for my final chapter. Still, on the inside, I was afraid that I might fail and my entire career would be an embarrassment.

Workouts started back up, and coach Moffitt was determined to get the best out of the 2012 team. We had big shoes to fill, and positions were up for grabs. Just because I was a senior didn't mean getting the first shot at a starting spot. I had the experience and technique to be a top contender, but so did a handful of other guys. Coach Moffitt wanted me to step up and become a vocal leader, but I wasn't so sure. I lacked confidence in myself and had built up a towering wall to climb in my head.

One day at a spring workout, I was in a mid-morning group. I was the oldest guy in the group, and Moffitt told me to break it down. "Me?" I thought to myself. Wow, he has never called on me for this honor. So, I raised my hand and said, "Hard work on three! — three!" Traditionally, one counts to three, and the rest of the group screams hard work. But for some reason, I thought I would skip one and two and jump straight to three. This was not uncommon. I mean, players do this from time to time. But this group had young guys who had never heard it done this way. So only about half of the players said hard work while the other half looked dumbfounded.

Well, Moffitt had taken a step or two away, and when he heard this lackluster breakdown, he whipped around and went ahead to chew me out in front of the group. I was embarrassed and angry at myself. What was wrong with me? Why didn't I just say one, two, three? I was not intentionally trying to be a class clown, but it looked that way to Moffitt. At that point, I knew I had to get my act together, or I would never get a chance to start.

A couple of weeks later, Moffitt had the team preparing for fourth quarter drills and had set up stations in the indoor facility so we could practice. I was running an L drill, and just as I planted my foot to make a turn, I felt a pop in my right calf. I limped through the finish line and went straight into the training room. I told Jack what I had felt, and they inspected my right calf.

To make a long story short, I visited with a couple of different doctors, and they discovered that I had torn my calf muscle. I have had rough injuries over the years, but this was the most challenging physical issue I had in my football career. I could not bear any weight on my right leg for two weeks. I had to use crutches to get to and from class. Jack told me that a torn calf was a nasty injury. My timeline for a full recovery was four to six weeks if I did not have any significant setbacks.

I showed concern on the outside, but on the inside, I was rejoicing! This meant I would have to sit out for the whole fourth quarter program! "Wow, what a blessing," I thought to myself. I was one of the best linemen at fourth quarter drills; I had some of the fastest times and best footwork of anybody on the team that year. But I still hated the concept of getting up at 5:30 a.m. and running drills and sprints until I nearly fainted. I would, of course, still get up with the team and take part in stretching. But, instead of running drills, I would pedal a bike on the sideline while having a front-row seat to watch everybody suffer. I would slowly pedal that bike and think so this was what it was like to be a coach getting a little pleasure out of watching pain and suffering.

After four weeks, my calf felt better, and Jack encouraged me to try drills. The team was on the last week of the fourth quarter program. I ran out that morning to stretch, and Moffitt started giving me a hard time about skipping nearly all of fourth quarter. I didn't enjoy him chastising me, but no doubt I deserved it. Moffitt is a motivator by trade, and if he ever stops yelling at you, that is when you really need to worry. I had finally realized this by that point in my LSU career.

After stretches, every player sprinted to their stations and prepared for an hour of torture. It didn't take long to realize my calf wasn't quite healed. My first station that day was Moffitt's, and when I jumped up to sprint through the line, my calf burst into pain. I never checked up. I limped straight back into the training room, glanced at Jack, and shook my head. Back on the bike, I went. I rehabbed my calf every day for another two weeks.

By that time, the team had started spring practice. I was not cleared to suit up, but I got tired of the same old rehab routine. Jack thought I may be ready to give it another go on week six. So, I dressed out in a green jersey, which meant little to no contact. It felt good to be back in pads. I always did well in spring practices; it was the regular season where I seemed to have the most trouble. I started off standing in during pulling drills. I was standing in the defensive end position, and 70 pulled around to mimic blocking me. He got a little carried away, and we bumped heads pretty good.

Bam, there it was again. I felt concussion symptoms. This would be my seventh concussion in five years. I was confused; it had been nearly two months since I had contact, and a slight head bump now made me feel cloudy. I didn't say anything about this at the time. it wasn't that bad, but it wasn't normal either.

We got to the team's part of practice, and the competition was fierce. We were in full pads, and guys were in a dogfight for starting positions. There were a couple of open spots on the offensive line, so Coach Stud gave everybody reps. I still wasn't fully cleared for this portion of practice, so I just stood and watched.

Left guard was an open spot, and guys were rotating. This was the position I would be fighting for that season as well. The younger guys kept making mistake after mistake, and Coach Stud was frustrated. After more than he could take, he turned to look at me and asked if I could take a couple of plays. Of course, I agreed. I was also tired of watching these guys make mistakes.

I jumped in the huddle, and zone extra was called (run play to the right). My job was to combo the block with the left tackle to the backside linebacker. I could run this play in my sleep. I made a quick step on the snap with my right foot, squatted for power, dropped my left shoulder, and drove it into the three-technique defensive tackle. I then thrust my hips to lift his shoulders and stop penetration so my left tackle could make contact and start driving. The goal was to push the defensive tackle vertically up field to create a backside lane for the running back. We did this to perfection on that rep. We moved him vertically up the field and straight into the backside linebacker and made a hole wide enough for a truck to drive through. But it was too good to be true. Just as we reached the backside linebacker, my calf popped again. I finished the play and then limped back over to the sidelines.

Coach Stud told the other guys rotating at left guard that I could block better on one leg than they could on two (Oh, the irony now!). I was not impressed. Like I said, I could do that with my eyes closed by that point in my career. My problem was never the run blocking technique. My problem would turn out to be between my ears. I would not come to realize this until years later.

I went into the training room and told Jack my calf popped again. He rolled his eyes and said, "Let's give it another week." Weeks earlier, Jack and I discussed his concern with the number of concussions I had had up to that point. He recommended that I stop playing if I had another bad one. He said it was my decision, but he was concerned about my life after football if these concussions continued.

Our conversation had been running through my mind, and I started to consider the thought of hanging up my cleats for good. It didn't seem like a bad option for me at the time. I mean, instead of having to take a chance of never living up to expectations, I could explain to people that injuries took my career from me. At the time, my just-turned-twenty-three-year-old self didn't know that this was a trick, and I would regret this decision for the remainder of my life. I thought I would get over it once I got into the real world, got a job, a house, a family, and had much more to live for. But I have all of that now, and this one decision continues to haunt me.

The next afternoon was terrible. We had an off day but still had a team meeting and watched film from the last practice. I had no idea what I was walking into. I was sitting in my assigned seat on the front row when Coach Miles burst through the door like a man on a mission. I could tell he had ugly news to air out. He started talking about practice and our progress and what he liked and didn't like. Then he changed gears to school.

Coach Miles would get a weekly report from the academic advisors full of conduct violations and players who were not making their grades. Well, apparently, my name was in that report for skipping classes. And to make matters worse, my teacher was the one who turned me in. Mine was not the only name on that list, but he had made up his mind that I would be the one he chewed out in front of the team. He lit into me, and I felt ashamed and humiliated. After he was done, he named all the players he wanted to meet with personally in his office. I was obviously on that list.

Never in my career had I been called out in a meeting like that. I mean, it was nothing new; he typically called out a player every week. But I never thought I would be that guy. I made my grades and never missed or was late to a meeting, practice, or workout. I had never been in serious trouble, except for that time 88, 47, and I were reprimanded for shooting at squirrels on campus with a BB gun. The police got called, and we nearly got kicked out of school, but I will save that story for another time.

The players whose names were called slowly made the long walk up the stairs to Coach Miles's office. One by one, we were called in to talk. I was the last name called. I figured he was saving the best butt chewing for last. I stepped in and sat down across from him. To my surprise, he was calm, cool, and collected. He looked up and asked if I was doing ok in a soft voice.

I was caught off guard by the question.

I was expecting a tongue lashing, but instead, the man showed compassion and caring, almost like a father. He said, "I know this isn't typical for you; something is bothering you." So, I told him how my injury had me depressed, and it felt like I was going nowhere. I just couldn't stay healthy, and my time was almost up. He nodded, gave fatherly advice, and dismissed me to go to my position meeting room. I walked out and thought, "Wow, I sure didn't see that coming."

Initially, I was mad that he made such a big show in front of the team, but my anger soon became compassion. Did this man genuinely care for my well-being? I believe he did. Coach Miles had many flaws, like we all do, but I will always say I think he truly cared for his players' well-being.

I walked back downstairs to the offensive line meeting room, sat down, and didn't say anything. I was in deep thought. I was fighting a battle in my head on whether I truly wanted to still be there on the team. I had a way out, and I knew it. Having a way out of doing something difficult is a dangerous tool for a man to possess. Often, a man will choose the easiest path, and I was simply that, a young dumb man.

Later I went home, and I couldn't get the thought of turning in my pads out of my head. I thought about it for days until I decided that I did not want to risk having another severe concussion. So, the next day I walked into Jack's office and told him at practice days prior, I had made head-to-head contact with another player, and I felt minor concussion symptoms. All of this was true. I told him I was done, and I didn't want to risk further complications involving my brain. He said, "Alright, well, let's go upstairs and discuss this decision with Coach Miles." I agreed, and away we went.

Jack told me to drop in and tell Coach Stud while he had a private conversation with Coach Miles. Talking to Coach Stud wasn't very difficult. He agreed that the rest of my life was more important and told me he was ok with my decision if I was.

After a few minutes, Jack knocked on the door and motioned me to walk to Coach Miles's office. I sat down and gave him my reasons, and he nodded his head and listened. He told me he thought that I could contribute to the team this season, but he realized it was my decision and left it all up to me in the end. I told him my mind was made up. I thanked him for everything he had done for me these past five years and for allowing me to play at LSU. Then we shook hands, and I walked out of his office.

Immediately I felt a weight was lifted off me. I had been kicking this decision around for weeks, and I had finally done it. I walked with Jack back down to the training room, and he told me I still needed to come to rehab every day until my calf was healed. I agreed and went ahead to do my rehab routine. When I finished, I walked by the weight room and wrestled with the thought of telling Moffitt about what I had done. In the end, I decided not to go talk to him. At the time, I convinced myself he would find out soon enough, and he didn't need to hear it from me. But more likely, I was just afraid of what he might say.

I have the utmost respect for Tommy Moffitt. He is the coach I spent the most time with during my five years as a player, and he told me things I still carry with me to this day. He taught me about life, hard work, and all things fitness. Those memories with Coach Moffitt are on replay in my head, and I will forever cherish them. One of my biggest regrets is not talking with him about my decision to take a medical before I made it. He may have advised me to reconsider and talked sense into me. But I will never know the answer to that question.

My life became ever so simple after that. I lived like an actual college kid with no real responsibilities and free time on my hands. I spent most of my time playing golf with 12. He was training for pro day, and after his daily workout, we would go play eighteen holes. 47 was still playing football, and he had to watch me sleep in, skip class, play golf, and drink a twelve-pack before bed every night. He often said he was jealous of me and wished he could do the same. But deep down, I was growing more jealous of him every day.

College life for me was like a new truck. It's all clean and fresh at first, and you absolutely love it. Then it gets a little age and becomes just a truck. But that bill keeps coming every month, and before long, you wish you would have just kept driving your old truck.

My dad suggested that I stay involved with the team and assist the assistant coaches or something along those lines. I thought that would be a good idea when the season started, but right now, I was going to have a little me time.

The season rolled around, and if I was going to stay involved with the team, I better get off my butt and do something. I still had six hours of credits before I could graduate, so since I would be in Baton Rouge for the fall, I might as well do something with my time.

Truthfully, I was scared to relive my past and stay involved with the football program. What if I started to regret my decision? What if the other guys on the team were disappointed or thought differently about me now? What if they thought the coaches dismissed me from the team and didn't give me a choice?

One day I worked up the courage to call Coach Stud and tell him I wanted to help him in any way I could. He said, "Yeah, sure. Come by this afternoon, and we will talk." I was so nervous I started taking shots of Taaka vodka beforehand. I probably took three or four shots before I worked up the courage to drive to Football Ops. The vodka taste was lingering, so I ate a bunch of breath mints before I walked into the building.

First, I stopped by the weight room to see who was around and got a chance to catch up with my old weight trainer for a minute. Moffitt wasn't around, and a part of me was glad. I didn't know what he would think about me, and honestly, I was scared to ask him.

I walked upstairs and knocked on the offensive staff room door. A voice said, "Come in," and I stepped through the doorway. When I stepped past the wooden door, I quickly noticed every offensive coach was sitting at the table. They all were glad to see me and asked me how I had been doing. I said I was good and asked how fall camp went. They said it was good and gave brief comments about the season and the team. I told them I wanted to stay involved and help them with whatever they needed me to. Coach Stud said, "Yea, sounds great. Just come by my office any time, and I'll find something for you." We then said our goodbyes, and I walked out of the door. That was the last time I would step foot on the Football Ops facility for four years. I went home, finished the bottle of Taaka vodka I had started earlier, and passed out.

For the rest of that semester, I did precisely what college students are known for, absolutely nothing. I only had two classes, and both were on Tuesdays and Thursdays. The three other days of the week, I slept in, smoked weed, and watched the whole series of Breaking Bad. Sometimes I would get hammered drunk at night if I wanted to change my routine up a little. Even though I only had class two days a week, I never went. The only time I showed up was to take a test or give a presentation, and I made a 3.0.

I watched all the football games on TV that season and secretly rooted for them to lose. Since I had left the team, I didn't want them to win any championships because I would surely regret my decision then. I still did not have a job lined up about midway through the semester, and I was doing less than I was at the beginning of the semester.

There came a point when I fell into a dark depression. I seriously started to fear that I would wake up and try to kill myself one day. I would fall into thoughts that my life's purpose had passed me by, and I did nothing at all to fight for it.

Every college player believes deep down that they are destined to play in the NFL and live a lavish life. I was no different. I had big dreams about life as an NFL player and did not think about what I would do if that didn't work out for me. Then as quickly as my opportunity had come, I had given it up. I quit.

Dreams will never work unless you do.

Even though I am not proud of these LSU stories, I tell them because they made me the man I am today, a man capable of reaching the darkest depths a person can imagine and have the strength and courage to never quit fighting.

Playing at LSU taught me how to fight. In a way, I owe my life to the LSU football program. Even though I didn't deserve it, they supported me throughout my playing career and during my most significant time of need in the hospital. Former and current coaches, players, and staff offered support and encouragement when I needed it the most. I know for a fact I would not be where

I am today if it wasn't for LSU's embracing culture and willingness to take care of their own. Once a tiger, always a tiger.

The LSU program is not only in the business of making great football players, but they are also in the business of making great men capable of facing life's toughest challenges.

Failure brings us to a place we never want to be again. Without my failures, I could not have begun to navigate the treacherous path life had taken me on.

CHAPTER 23
A New Way Forward

The day had finally come when it was time to travel to Chicago. Liana and Barrett were coming along for the trip, so we had the Suburban loaded down with bags. Barrett had never been on that long a road trip, so we decided to split the drive in half. After lunch, we would leave Monroe, drive the first half, stay the night, wake up, and drive the last half the following morning. There aren't many places to stay exactly halfway between Monroe and Chicago. We could have stayed in Memphis, but this was a little less than halfway, and to be fair to Barrett, I picked a spot closer to the middle.

When we arrived in Blytheville, Arkansas, I told Liana this was where we would stay for the night. She was not happy with me. Liana won't tell you this herself, but she is a city girl through and through. She will have nothing to do with it if there isn't the right amount of glitz and glamour. Well, Blytheville was missing the glitz and glamour. I personally didn't think it was that bad. We were right on the interstate staying at a Hampton Inn nestled between Shell Food Mart and Terry-Thomas Ford. There seemed to be decent places to eat, and I saw nothing wrong. But she told me she was not staying there and to keep driving. So, I pulled up the map and showed her that what was left between here, and Chicago wasn't much better than Blytheville.

Against her wishes, we stayed in Blytheville for the night.

We got up early and finished the drive to Chicago the following day. Neither Liana nor I had ever been to the Windy City, and we were looking forward to seeing the sights. After we checked in, the first thing we did was find a park so Barrett could release pent-up energy from the car ride. After the park, we rode by David's office to know how to get there in the morning. I can't lie; I wasn't too impressed at first sight. It was in an old shopping center, and the windows were mirror tinted. There wasn't even a sign on the door. All we could find was plain lettering on the community shopping center billboard that said David Rotter Prosthetics. I thought, "I sure hope we didn't make a mistake coming all the way up here," but as the old saying goes, looks can be deceiving.

When we pulled up at David's the next morning, he ran outside to greet me.

"Look at this skinny guy! How was the drive up?" he asked. We hit it off at once. I couldn't help but notice that David had this same connection with all his patients. He walked me in and introduced me to his staff. David didn't waste any time. We got to work immediately. First, he measured me for his patented hippie garment. Then he cast me for my socket. This process took all the first morning. After that, he encouraged me to stick around and visit with other patients.

I met fascinating people in the lounge at Rotter Prosthetics. I met courageous veterans, paralympic athletes, a former NFL player, young amputees, old amputees, grandmas, grandpas, husbands, wives, fathers, mothers, sons, and daughters. I call them friends and mentors I look up to. Meeting all these people and hearing their stories of what they had been through and overcome gave me hope that I could do the same.

The next day David finished my check socket. The socket is the part of the prosthetic that attaches to my body. The check socket is used to dial in the perfect fit. Once the check socket is finished, that mold is used to make the actual socket attached to the prosthetic. This is the most critical part of building a prosthetic. If the socket is not created right, the user will experience pain and discomfort. This will ultimately make walking more difficult.

Once the check socket fit perfectly, David let me go for the day. He explained it would take the rest of that day and the following day to build the socket. So, I showed up just after lunch the next day, and the first thing David said to me was, "Are you ready to walk?"

I said, "Hell yeah!"

He told me he would assemble my leg, and hopefully, I would be able to put it on that afternoon. So, Liana, Barrett, and I hung out and chatted with some other patients.

Barrett was one at the time, and he was also learning to walk. In what world are a thirty-year-old father and his one-year-old son learning to walk simultaneously?

To this day, it is still hard for me to believe this is my actual life. Nobody ever expects or thinks they will lose a limb and become an amputee. All the hours I spent dreaming of how my life might turn out, and not one second of those thoughts revolved around becoming an amputee.

Late that afternoon, David finished assembling my prosthetic leg. David built my prosthesis from scratch in three days. At the time, I didn't understand how insane that was. Now that I have more experience and have worked with other practitioners, I am in awe of his rare talent. And to be fair to his staff, he didn't do it all by himself. They help with the steps of the process.

When David walked out holding that four-foot-long hunk of metal and carbon fiber, I thought he may have robbed it from an alien spaceship. This thing was wild-looking. Because I have a hip disarticulation, my prosthetic replaces three working joints, the hip, knee, and ankle.

And because I am 6'6, this was the biggest prosthetic David had ever built.

He went over how it worked, then handed it to me to put on. Well, he two-handed it because it weighs fifteen pounds. He told me I needed to get it as tight as possible while still breathing. "This will give you better control," he explained.

When I put it on, my first thought was that I had a broomstick dangling from my body. It felt nothing like a leg. This was a foreign object, and I had no idea how I would walk. David showed me the technique and motioned me to take it for a spin.

An adequately aligned hip disarticulation prosthetic should work with minimal effort. The goal is to stand up straight, eyes forward. Take a step with your sound leg while keeping your chest and shoulders upright. At that point, the leg should go through the swing phase and land a step out in front. You then drop your weight down onto the prosthetic and repeat.

Sounds easy enough, right?

That first steps were terrifying. It was not easy to trust that weird-looking leg. I could not feel it moving, so I had to literally walk on faith. I had to let go of control and trust that David built the leg in a way so it would not break when I dropped all my weight onto it. At that time, I was not used to putting my faith in something completely out of my control.

It took me dozens of attempts to get the feeling down. I was walking inside parallel bars to grab one if I started to fall. After about a hundred trips back and forth in the bars, I got brave enough to take a few steps with no support. With two people by my side, I started to walk back and forth across the room. Within an hour of putting the prosthetic on for the first time, I walked with no assistance (I have the video for proof). David was shocked at how fast I learned to walk. I made a couple of trips back and forth across the room, and I started to get cocky.

I walked a little faster when David told me to slow down and walk smoother. Suddenly, wham! I was on the floor. It happened so fast that it took me a moment to realize I had fallen. One second, I'm walking. The next, I'm sprawled out on the floor. I turned to look at David, expecting him to be concerned. He wasn't. He said, "Look, man, that's just going to happen sometimes."

I then realized this would be much harder than I thought. I never considered falling that big of an issue, but now that I had done it, I was a little spooked. My violent crash tore the leg all up, so David suggested I head back to the hotel and start fresh tomorrow.

That night the realization of what I had just accomplished sunk in. I had walked for the first time in six months. I went to bed with a smile on my face and hope for my future. I hadn't felt that much confidence and excitement since I received my scholarship to play for LSU.

FLASHBACK:
ZERO TO HERO

I started playing football in fourth grade. I played running back and linebacker. I was one of the biggest and fastest in my class in grade school. This worked to my advantage in sports. I made all-stars in baseball every year and was one of my pee-wee football team's leading rushers and tacklers.

As I got into middle school, my classmates began to pass me up in speed. I was still the tallest in my class, but my athleticism lagged far behind my size. Even though my classmates had caught up or passed me, I managed to stay competitive. I was still the best baseball pitcher in my grade. Because of this, baseball was my favorite sport.

I continued to play football, but my running back and linebacker days were over. I now played tight end and defensive end. I struggled tremendously on the football field from seventh to ninth grade. I have one story to sum up my skill level during those years.

In my ninth-grade year, the team traveled to Jackson, Mississippi, to play Madison Ridgeland. We only had seventeen guys on the high school football team from twelfth through ninth grade. I was playing left tackle, a position I had no business being in. I was 6'4, 200 pounds, rocking a body shaped like a pear.

It was the second quarter, and we were getting crushed. Madison Ridgeland had three times the number of kids, and we were dropping like flies. The down was fourth and long. We were backed up close to our end zone, so we chose to punt. Due to an injury, I was placed on the punt team the day before at practice. Well, due to my lack of awareness, the change slipped my mind.

Just before the snap of the ball, the coach next to me on the sideline started screaming, "Wait! Wait! We are missing our left guard!" By then, it was too late, the ball was snapped, and one of Madison Ridgeland's players shot through the line and blocked the punt. A second Madison Ridgeland player knocked our punter clean out (who happened to be the best player on the team), while a third Madison Ridgeland player scooped and scored. When the ball was snapped, I realized that I was the missing left guard. Standing next to me, my coach hung his head and pulled his red Raiders pride cap down over his face. He seemed to be on the verge of a mental breakdown.

Suddenly he lifted his head, his voice cracking as he screamed out, "Who is supposed to be at left guard?"

I leaned in close to his ear and mumbled, "Uh, I think that's supposed to be me, Coach." He turned, gave me a nightmarish look of utter dissatisfaction and shame, turned on a dime, and stormed off down the sideline to get as far away from me as possible.

This story paints a clear picture of my football playing abilities from seventh to ninth grade; too tall, awkward, and goofy to be of any use. Lucky for me, this trend wouldn't last.

Toward the end of my ninth-grade year at Riverfield, we decided that my brother and I would change schools. We thought I could play college baseball and felt I would get more exposure at a bigger school.

My brother and I enrolled at Sterlington High School in 2005. We moved to Monroe and started living with our mom. We had lived under my dad's roof eighty percent of the time since birth, and he had kept a tight leash on us growing up. We were given more slack when we flip-flopped this percentage under our mom's roof. This allowed my social life to blossom at Sterlington High school.

I soon got the reputation of a frequent partygoer from my coaches. I enjoyed having a good time and partying hard on the weekends, but I was no hell-raising wild child. I continued to focus my energy on sports. I had plans to play football at Sterlington High school, but my focus was pitching for the baseball team.

I made a big jump from my ninth to tenth-grade year in football. I played tight end, and I had a decent year changing schools and competition levels.

Sterlington is a much bigger school than Riverfield and plays in the Louisiana Highschool Athletic Association. It was a 2A school and had built a strong football program.

At the end of my tenth-grade year, I received second-team all-district honors. I was in disbelief I had made all-district. My old Riverfield coaches would not believe this. They were against my move to Sterlington and told me I would never amount to anything if I transferred. I was "not good enough" to play at a bigger school. These words stung when I heard them, but it turns out that I would get the last laugh.

After football season that year, I partied a little too hard, and my baseball coach noticed. I was expecting to pitch for the baseball team that season, but my coach had other plans. I strolled into those first few practices like a top dog, but he quickly cut me down to size. He had me shagging balls and running bases while the starters hit BP and fielded. Instead of talking to my coach about the situation, I chose to take the low road and acted as if I didn't care. This was all for show. Deep down, I did care. I wanted to contribute so badly that season. I held all my feelings inside and grew angrier by the day. Sound familiar to my LSU story?

Spring football started the week after baseball season ended. I was looking forward to putting my disappointing baseball season behind me and blowing off steam. This just so happened to work perfectly to my advantage. That year, 88 would be a senior on the team. Several top colleges were recruiting him around the country. He was a tall, rangy receiver who could run like the wind blows. He had racked up gaudy stats his junior season, and colleges took notice.

When coaches came to watch 88 play that spring, they couldn't help but notice me, a 6'6, 230-pound, big-framed tight end running all over the field, blocking like a madman. Because I was so upset about baseball season, I lost my mind that year in spring football practice.

After our spring game, college coaches came up and asked me for my information and told me I would be hearing from them. I was in utter disbelief. I never expected that my path to playing college sports would be football. Just two years earlier, I was an embarrassment to the game of football. Now here I was, getting recruited by SEC schools. I quickly forgot about my baseball woes and focused my sights on the upcoming football season.

I balled out my junior season. My receiving stats weren't enormous by any means, but they were respectable. Our offense was geared more toward the run, and I spent most of my time blocking for our two-stud running backs.

I received honors following my junior season and was named First-Team All-District and First-Team All-State. I got my first scholarship offer from Ole Miss a couple of weeks after the season. In the months to come, I would receive over twenty scholarship offers from schools all over the country.

LSU sent me an invite to their annual Junior Day. On a cool, cloudy Saturday in February, my dad drove me down to Baton Rouge to partake in the festivities. LSU had not offered me a scholarship at that point, and I wasn't positive if I would get one from them.

We wined and dined and got a grand tour of all the impressive facilities. Then they brought all the recruits over to watch the men's basketball game that was being played in the PMAC.

On our way to the game, tight end Coach Josh Henson pulled my dad and me aside and said, "Coach Miles would like to see you all in his office." My dad and I were caught off guard. Could this be it? Was LSU going to give me a scholarship?

I still wasn't convinced when I walked through the big door of Coach Miles's office. The office was decorated with all kinds of memorabilia from past LSU teams and some of his stuff from his playing days at Michigan.

He sat us down in oversized purple chairs, and the first words out of his mouth were, "We are giving you a scholarship." His words seemed to echo around the room and throughout my head as the unbelievable news sank in.

I could not believe my ears. As a kid, I grew up cheering on the LSU football team. I attended games and dreamed of running out of that stadium tunnel onto the field. Now I was sitting with the head coach, and he allowed me to do just that. I became so lost in thought that I don't rightly remember what all else we talked about. All I could think at that moment was my life would be changed forever.

We finished our conversation, then said our goodbyes. I think they really wanted me to commit that day. But the recruiting process only happens once in a lifetime, and I wanted to check out other schools while I had the chance. My LSU offer wasn't going anywhere, and I wanted to have a little more fun before deciding. The other schools I visited that spring were Ole Miss, Auburn, Alabama, and LA Tech. I was pretty much dead set on going to LSU, but I wasn't ready to get married just yet. I was having too much fun checking out the other pretty girls.

I didn't have to try very hard to make good grades in high school. I never brought a book home to study between my tenth and twelfth grades at Sterlington. My GPA in high school was 3.5.

One day that spring, I was in algebra class, and I finished my work early. I laid my head down on my desk and dozed off. My teacher sat me in the very back of the classroom because I had behavioral issues.

Suddenly I was awakened by a loud banging on the blue metal classroom door. I lifted my head and felt a little dazed and confused. When I looked toward the door, my high school head coach looked at me. He said, "You mind if I steal the sleeping giant from you?" My teacher shook her head no. I rolled my eyes and thought he would scold me for sleeping in class. I just knew I had a red circle on my forehead from lying on my algebra book, and my eyes hadn't entirely adjusted to the bright fluorescent light. When I went to stand up, I stumbled and nearly fell to the ground. My leg was dead asleep, and I had no feeling in it. I limped to the door, obviously annoyed that I had been awakened from my afternoon nap. As I stepped out into the hall, I perked up at once.

The LSU tight end coach Josh Henson stood with a confused smirk on his face. I tried to hide my limp and cover my red forehead as I stepped forward to shake his hand. He asked me, "Are you hurt?" while trying not to burst into laughter. I fessed up and told him my leg was asleep and that he had caught me napping. We chatted briefly, then he told me to go back to class.

I hobbled back through the classroom door and sat at my desk. I had never been so embarrassed in my life. I feared they might pull my scholarship on account of character flaws. At the time, I wasn't too happy with myself. Now I look back on this and can't help but laugh.

I thought it would be best to commit before my senior football season started. If the unthinkable happened, and I had a career-ending injury, the school that held my commitment would honor my scholarship. So, after begging and pleading from my dad, I decided it was time to pull the trigger.

June rolled around, and I told Dad I had made my decision. I would play for LSU. Even a blind man could have seen that coming. I called up Coach Henson and told him I was coming down for a visit later that week. He sounded excited on the phone and poked me for my reason, but I didn't spill the beans. I wanted to commit in person.

When we arrived at Football Ops, we got straight down to business. We were greeted at the door and escorted straight to Coach Miles's office. He already knew what this was about; he had seen this hundreds of times. We sat down in those same big purple chairs where I got the news of my scholarship, and I told him that I was committing to play for the Tigers. He shouted for joy and reached out to shake my hand. He then gave me a wink and said, "I knew you were going to be a Tiger. I was never worried."

We then had a brief discussion about what the next steps were. He told me to enjoy my senior season, and even if I got hurt, my scholarship was safe. This was music to my dad's ears. I think he was already counting the fortune he would save on college tuition. We stepped out of Coach Miles's impressive office and met with Coach Henson. We talked ball for about half-hour before our stomachs started rumbling. Coach Henson said we would have time for this later and to go and celebrate. We left with our heads held high and went to eat at Walk-Ons on the edge of campus.

As a recruit, I got tickets to every home game. I didn't miss one during the 2007 national championship season. They let the recruits onto the field for pregame warmups. The energy of

100,000 fans steadily filling the stadium around me was the most incredible high I had ever experienced.

Just before kickoff at the Auburn game, I walked off the sideline to find my seat in the stands. I was walking up the stadium stairs with other recruits. Suddenly, I felt somebody grab my arm and pull me. When I turned my head to see who was pulling, I saw a beautiful dark-haired girl in a low-cut purple tank top. She pulled me in close and gave me a kiss on the lips. I could taste the Sprite and Malibu Rum on her breath. She pulled away and screamed at the top of her lungs, "WHEWWW! Come to LSU!" Everybody who saw this started cheering and chanting "LSU, LSU!"

Welcome to the jungle, young man, where the tiger is king (Of course, this happened before I ever dated the love of my life, Liana)!

I felt like I was on top of the world. I had spent so many hours dreaming of this moment as a child, and here I was, getting to live out my dream. I thought back to all those who doubted me years prior. Now the tables had finally turned.

CHAPTER 24
The Gift

The next day in Chicago was filled with walking. I walked back and forth across David's office all morning. By lunch, it was time for a break. Initially, I was supposed to use a mechanical knee. The mechanical knee requires you to have sound technique. If your technique is poor while using it, you will fall. David watched me walk around the office that day and thought I may be ready for the microprocessor knee (C-Leg). The C-Leg has sensors in the foot and knee that can adjust the resistance in a split second, depending on what kind of terrain it's on. It also has a stumble assist feature, so if you happen to take a wrong step, the knee will give you a chance to recover, while the mechanical knee will plant you in the dirt.

I often describe the C-Leg to people as the smartest thing in the room. What I like about it is the confidence it gives me. I don't care who you are; wrong steps will happen. I know I can catch myself if it does its job, and I have yet to experience a time when it hasn't.

Before David would agree to upgrade me, he wanted me to walk outside. "You mean on the hard concrete?" I said,

"Yep, you got to do it; that's the only way you are getting this C-Leg, man," he explained.

So out the door, I went. I was terrified about walking outside. The last thing I wanted to do was fall and injure myself. But because David had confidence in me, I pressed on. I walked circles around the parking lot, weaving in and out of parked cars. Before long, I had done several laps, and David said, "Alright, I've seen enough. You're ready for the C-Leg."

Because the components are different, it took half the next day to properly attach and align the C-Leg. By that afternoon, it was ready for me to take it for a spin. It took me a little while to get the hang of the new knee. This thing felt different and was a little heavier than the mechanical knee, but I got my rhythm back eventually. Since it was Friday, David let me take the prosthetic to the hotel to practice over the weekend.

When we arrived back at the hotel, I asked the receptionist to take a family picture. I bent down and picked up Barrett and held him in my arms, standing for the first time in six months. This was an extraordinary moment for my family.

For so long, I didn't know if I would ever be able to hold Barrett in my arms while standing again. While in the hospital, I mostly thought about the big things in life I would miss out on. After getting home, I realized far more little things were taken away from me, and in the end, these were the things that hurt the most. It is hard for people to appreciate how incredible the human body truly is.

Since my new body is not made for this world, every aspect of my old life that I took for granted now sticks out like a sore thumb: cooking dinner, mowing the grass, chasing Barrett around the house, going for a walk, carrying a cup of coffee or plate of food, moving furniture around, grocery shopping, taking out the trash, trick or treating, bike riding, carrying chairs to the beach, playing catch, and so many more things. I had to adapt or change everything in my life. This was just as much a mental burden as it was physical.

The following day Liana suggested we go to Chicago. I agreed and decided I would wear my leg. I soon found out that wearing my leg at David's shop and wearing it out in public were worlds apart. We picked Navy Pier for our first stop. Looking back, I don't know if I was crazy or plain foolish about what I was getting myself into. This was the first day I had used my prosthetic outside the comfort and safety of David's supervision. I was all on my own now, and I was going to walk down Navy Pier on a beautiful Saturday in May!

There were cars and people everywhere when we arrived. It took us ages to find a parking space, and as luck would have it, we were nowhere near the pier. Liana grabbed Barrett and loaded him in the stroller as I took a couple of deep breaths and focused on the task at hand.

"Jedi, Jedi, Jedi," I repeatedly said in my head. This was David's keyword for me when I needed to focus on keeping my chest and shoulders upright. We slowly made our way down Navy Pier and stopped at Jimmy Buffets Margaritaville to eat lunch. I sat down and let out a big sigh of relief. "I can do this," I thought. I had probably walked a quarter of a mile so far and felt great.

After burgers and fries, Liana wanted to take Barrett to the children's museum on the pier. We walked in, bought tickets, and found a corner to set down our stuff. Every kid in the place was staring daggers at me.

Kids are inquisitive when they see a prosthetic. They just blurt out whatever is on their mind. It is best for any amputees out there to have prepared statements for mouthy kids. My favorite line is telling the kid I didn't eat my vegetables, and one day it just fell off. Parents don't mind this one so much, either.

Blocking out stares and what people may think has been one of the hardest things for me to deal with as an amputee. I worry that strangers are nervous or on edge around me and keep their distance and mouths closed in public places. Thoughts pop into my head that I am grotesque-looking to strangers. I worry that my kids will receive unwanted questions or be picked on because of my disability.

Far too often, my thoughts grow dark, and I feel helpless and bitter about my circumstance. I must spend countless hours working on my mental state and armor-plating my daily mindset. Over time I have begun to see things differently, which I will share.

I have come to realize losing my leg is a gift.

But it is not a gift for me. It is a gift to everybody else. I am the person in charge of giving it to people. I can wrap it up as pretty as I would like and hand it to as many people as I want. I do this by simply living life and continuing to wake up and take it one day at a time.

When people see me, their first reaction is curiosity, followed by pity. They look at me and can't imagine what I have been through and how difficult my life must be. They quickly notice the smile on my face and wonder if I know something they don't when they have two legs and struggle to smile. I have met many people with disabilities, and they can't get past the thought that this was a type of undeserving punishment and hardship placed on them for no reason.

I want you all to understand you have been given a great responsibility to share your gift with the world. Keep moving forward and getting better every day. You never know who may be watching you living your life and how that can be a light for someone.

It is one of my hopes that by sharing this, it will help someone else.

There are too many people out there trying their hardest to show everybody how wonderful and spectacular their lives are. They are bigger, faster, stronger, smarter, tougher, and wealthier than everybody else. We need more people willing to share their insecurities and failures in life, people who aren't afraid to be vulnerable and open about their struggles, and who are willing to share their whole story, not just the highlight reel. Life is hard, and it's okay because we are all here living it together!

I am more fearful of not being a part of my children's lives than receiving unwanted stares and uncomfortable questions.

Soon, Barrett started to melt down in the children's museum, and Liana dragged him out, kicking and screaming. I grabbed the stroller and met them back out front. It was about time for Barrett's nap, so we decided to head back to the car.

On the walk back, I began to feel fatigued. I had probably walked a mile by now, and I was suffering. There was quite a crowd on the pier. I had to weave in and out of people while trying to keep up. On one such weave, I felt my leg begin to give out. I had to scramble and hop a couple of times to catch my balance. "Jedi, Jedi, Jedi," I repeated.

We snapped a quick family picture, then loaded up in the suburban. I was wiped. I hadn't felt that tired since the 2015 all-night frog gigging competition.

We made a loop through downtown Chicago to see the sights. Barrett was sound asleep by then, so we decided to head back to the hotel. On the way back, David texted me to check-in. I told him we went to Navy Pier. His response was, "Dude, you are crazy! But I love it!" At the time, I didn't think it was that big of a deal, but now I think maybe I am a little crazy.

I laid low the next day, and Liana took Barrett shopping on the outskirts of Chicago. I needed a little time alone to process everything I had done. I was watching TV when I glanced over at my prosthetic. It started screaming at me to put it on and do a little walking. So, I wrestled it on and stepped out into the hall. I walked up and down the hall for an hour. The cleaning crew probably thought I was trying to steal their shampoo. But I don't think they were too threatened by me. At the speed I was walking, I wouldn't get very far.

I spent the rest of the following week at David's office practicing and talking to interesting people. When Thursday rolled around, we said our goodbyes and thanked David and his staff for everything they had done. David built the tool to help me gain a piece of my life back and gave me the knowledge and confidence to use it. It was now up to me to master walking. I would need to practice and wear the leg as much as possible to learn to live everyday life on it.

I got home, trained hard, and essentially mastered the art of walking with a four-foot prosthetic leg. I could go anywhere and do anything, just at a bit slower pace than I would like.

I thought walking would bring me freedom, peace, and joy, a deeper sense of what I was searching for in my new life of struggle. But I was mistaken. As grand and wonderful as I had played up walking would be, it still was nowhere near walking on two real legs. When you are missing an entire leg, life will just be hard. There's no way around it. I didn't want pain and suffering to be a part of my life anymore, so I took a shot at running from it. I can't run very fast these days, so it wasn't long until it caught back up to me.

CHAPTER 25

My Spiritual Enlightenment

Here I was again, back in the darkness of my circumstance, but new life always starts in the dark.

Coming out of this tragedy, I felt the need to reach out and help others who also were going through some sort of physical tragedy. Early on, I would say my approach was more of an "If I can do it, you can do it" kind of vibe. On the outside, I attempted to seem compassionate and understanding, but on the inside, I longed for a compliment to inflate my inner ego. I craved praise and compliments from anybody willing to give it. As far and wide as my story went, I tended to receive more than my fair share.

Deep down, I wanted the glory for facing my challenges head-on, for not backing down and ever pressing forward. Striving to inflate one's ego is an exhausting task, and on account of being on my last leg, I was worn out and searching for meaning and purpose in my difficult circumstance.

People were interested in my story and had begun to ask me to share it in all sorts of different ways: public speaking, podcast, news articles, and video clips. I was in awe of the responses I got when I shared parts of my journey, but I knew there was so much more than only a book could do my story justice. I had begun to think about what my story would look like in a book format. I even made attempts at writing one. But writing a book is HARD! My efforts ended in vain, and I was ready to give up on it.

Sudden spiritual enlightenment is a real thing.

I know it is real because I have encountered it. I have felt it vibrate my body as if I was holding onto railroad tracks as a train steamed by. And no, I wasn't in a concert; I wasn't in a mega-church worship service. I was eating sauce-covered ribs and baked beans from Podnuh's BBQ, sitting in my Chevrolet Z71 in the parking lot next to the Power Lube off 165 North.

In a moment of clarity, a rush of bliss flooded my spirit.

At that moment, I found the center from which everything flows. My mind raced; what I had been searching for was with me all along. It was with me as a young boy running with the wind on Fragala Street. It was with me as a young man coming into my own and skipping under the live oak trees on the LSU campus after my last final exam. It was with me as my newborn son entered the world, gasping for air. It was agape love, and it found me again on a warm afternoon with BBQ smeared on my face.

I wasn't looking for God, but he revealed himself to me.

I wasn't sure what to do with it, so I naturally scarfed down the beans and pulled back onto the highway. "Where am I going? What's wrong with me? Should I go to the doctor?" These were my first reactions. "Na dude, just go home. You're fine." I pulled up in the driveway, walked to my room, took my leg off, grabbed my crutches, and crutched to my office. I sat down at my computer and started typing. I typed for four days straight.

If you are reading this, then you have read every word I typed in those four days.

I am fully aware my life is insane; insanely odd, insanely hilarious, and insanely heartbreaking all at the same time. As the old saying goes, God works in mysterious ways. I experienced the point of no return, the edge of life. I can't think of a better way to wake somebody up and start the process of transformation, to live the life I was always supposed to live, the life we are all called to live: a life of service, a life of sacrifice, a life of love, a life devoted to the preservation of life itself.

I worship God because he gives me a life to be truly proud of and am thankful for the wisdom to know what makes life worth living.

Late one night, I could not sleep. I kept tossing and turning and eventually decided to grab my phone and write. I had been wanting to write a description of what it felt like to lose my leg and what I would face. These are the words that came to me:

One day a stranger comes up to you and says, "Alright, I'm about to take your leg, and you must hand over everything you know in your life without any questions. If you refuse, you will die. I will give you a new life now, but this life will be uncomfortable and full of suffering. You will believe you can't possibly do it, and you will want to quit.

It will help if you have patience, the right mindset, seek proven wisdom, and keep positive people around you in your new life. If you follow these instructions, you will have a better chance of truly living.

If you make it, one day far down the road, you will look back on all your suffering and be thankful for it. The suffering will give you a story to be proud of and make you a light so bright that others will flock to you and ask, "How can you be so happy? You're missing your leg!"

You will then reply, "How can you not be happy with two legs?"

You will learn so much about yourself fighting this battle, and one day you won't be able to imagine your life with your leg. You will wonder, "What would I have become if I would have never had to fight to stand?"

Who would have guessed that a life with a missing leg would parallel a life devoted to Christ, a life of giving with no expectation of receiving anything in return?

I mean, seriously, I can't make this stuff up. Go back and replace the word leg with sin, and this little piece applies to every living soul.

I cannot find a better target to point my life, a better example of a person than Jesus Christ. Show me another story that has stood the test of time, and no matter what opposition it faces, it always pushes through the pages of history. It is a story so deep that it is impossible to comprehend the vast number of hours people have spent contemplating it while it continues to feel truly alive among the people it transforms. Why would I not want to attach my name to the most famous story ever told? How else could I claim a place in history for all of eternity?

I have wondered countless times why it had to be this extreme.

An easy life doesn't make a good story. An easy life wouldn't boast the power of God. I remind myself that this is only temporary. One day, my suffering will end and give me a better hope that I will one day walk with ease again, free of this burden.

I have good days and bad days. But overall, I am grateful to have a day at all.

I have put much thought into what I am supposed to do with my life going forward. I feel strongly that I have been called to share my story in a way that may point others to the light, toward a life of virtue.

I often hear the phrase, "I couldn't live with myself if I did that." Let me tell you something; it's easy to live a rotten selfish life. I did it for years. What is hard is dying with a rotten, selfish life. I did that once, and I am not signing up to do that again.

I feel that a part of death is now stuck with me, and I think about dying every day. I think about how I will not die in peace because I achieved financial and material success. Please take it from my experience that at no point while I lay in the cold wet grass next to Hwy 465 did, I wish I had made more money. I did not wish I had a bigger house, a nicer truck, or owned more hunting property. I did not regret that I had not checked everything off my bucket list. I did not long for any material wealth or power whatsoever.

If it meant nothing to me then, what makes me so sure it's worth spending a lifetime to attain?

In what I thought were my last dying moments on earth, I didn't long for stuff. Instead, I longed for truth, love, and genuine relationships. And you know what, material wealth cannot buy you any of those things. The currency that will award you these things are time, service, and sacrifice. And it just so happens these things are distributed equally among everybody alive today.

You don't need to be wealthy to spend time or communicate with your loved ones. You don't need to be privileged to serve someone in need. And you don't need to have high social status to sacrifice your wants and desires for the greater good.

You have everything you need to live a virtuous life right now.

To be clear, there is nothing wrong with earning material success in life. You can have your cars, fancy house, and a fat bank role. But this pursuit alone is insufficient in creating a life to be deeply proud of. There is a better adventure calling out to us.

Do you, hear it?

Problems arise when we place material success or selfish pleasure above all else and are willing to step on or neglect others to grab hold of it without considering the implications. Deep down we all know this, but we have difficulty truly believing it.

Is it better to leave all your stuff behind to your loved ones, or all of yourself behind to them?

Because I was obsessed with the endless checklist of personal success, I feel I cannot stress this enough. I have been to death's doorstep and stared into the darkness of self-deception. No earthly possession is worth sacrificing your soul to attain. Christ told us this same thing 2,000 years ago.

Luke 9:25 says, "For what profit is it to a man if he gains the whole world, and is himself destroyed or lost?" (NKJV)?

I cannot rightly say if I ever would have truly believed these words unless I had seen them play out in my life.

Being a follower of Christ has helped me understand and take steps toward becoming the person I longed to be at the very moment I felt life slipping from my grasp.

It would take me writing another book to explain how I have come to this conclusion.

By no means have I perfected any of the virtues I have just laid out. But I can say with all my heart that for the first time in my life, I know which way is up. I have chosen to partake in the adventure of climbing from the valley of vice to ascending the mountain of virtue in hope of one day becoming closer to the light of the Son.

From this day until my last, I will share my story and experience with anyone out there who is willing to listen.

To God be the glory. Amen.

EPILOGUE

Liana

The first year after Matt's accident, I thought things would never be normal again. I woke up every morning and as I watched him exit our bedroom on crutches, it would hit me all over again that this really was our life now. I thought this realization would never go away until one morning, it did. I started waking up with thoughts of our day ahead vs flashbacks of the past.

There were many challenging days, and I would think to myself, God how are we going to do all of this? Nothing was as easy as it used to be, but that didn't mean it wasn't doable and it wasn't worth it. It took extra work on both of our parts to plan, anticipate obstacles, and most importantly keep a positive attitude. I know without a doubt, we couldn't have made it through this without our son.

> Barrett,
> We love you so much. You have always been wise beyond your years and God knew how perfect you would be for our family. From speaking six-syllable words at the age of one to mastering ten-year-old Harry Potter Lego kits at the age of five, you never cease to amaze us. You are hilarious and your humor has kept us smiling and on our toes since the day you were born. You never meet a stranger and make friends with everyone. You are so passionate about your interests. Spending time with you in

"your world" are some of the best memories we will treasure forever. You are and will always be our baby no matter how much bigger you get than Mommy! You've been through it all with us. I'll never forget about a year after the accident you finally realized something was different. We were sitting in the living room, and you looked over at Daddy and said in a perplexed tone, "You have one leg. You don't have two legs." You thought about this for a minute, flipped over the ottoman, and continued dancing to a song on TV. We followed your lead and kept the dance of life going, too. Thank you for being our Barrett. We are so very proud of who you are and who you have yet to become!

Love,
Mommy & Daddy

Right about when we felt like we had this new way of life sort of figured out, I began to long for our family to grow. I always wanted my children to be close in age and with Barrett already two, I knew my ideal age gap window was closing. We decided there would never be a perfect time with our situation, so we took a leap of faith and trusted that God would carry us through this next season of life.

Charlotte,
Our curly Auburn hair, baby girl. While most babies sleep their first few hours of life, you were wide awake and ready to interact. You made all kinds of faces in the hospital, and I told your daddy that you were going to be a funny girl and I was so right. You spent most of your first year watching your brother, longing to be able to do all that he could. You adored him and once you started walking, there was no stopping you or telling you no. You've always beat to the sound of your own drum, and

we love watching every second of it. You're our Goggi Girl! Our hearts melt when we watch you rocking the kitties like babies and nearly stop when we watch you jump and flip off the couch and land with a quick booty shake dance. Only you could be all of this in one, Charlotte Ann. We adore you and are so thankful God gave us you. These past two years have been an absolute joy watching you grow into your personality, and we know you are only getting started. Nothing can stop you, girl!

Love,
Mommy & Daddy

God has blessed our family in so many ways. Although this isn't the easiest path, it's changed the course of our family and future. For that, we'll be forever thankful. God has called us out of our comfort zones to live an intentional life of purpose. Though it took a life-altering accident to wake us up and change our perspective, everyone in this world is perfectly and uniquely made by God for an individual purpose. Somewhere, someone or something needs you. Share your light!

Thank you to all the doctors and nurses for everything you did-we will forever be grateful to you.

Thank you, David Rotter Prosthetics, for getting Matt back on his feet (literally) and back active in the world.

Thank you to our family, friends, and community for all your support through this time in our lives. We love you all so very much and couldn't have done this without each of you.

Matt

Some time has passed since this story took place and life continues to speed up. Barrett and Charlotte provide lots of entertainment around the house. Having children has helped me grow up, bear my suffering, and keep moving forward. I feel like they make me age and tire faster, while also keeping me young and energized. Yin and Yang, I guess. I'm sure other parents can understand that.

For generations now, parents have always said, "I want my kids to have more than I did."

Early in my parenthood, I considered more to be material. Now I see that more does not only mean the material but also the spiritual. I don't think my children will care what house they grew up in or the car they drive. They will care if I spend time with them, talk to them about things that matter, and show and tell them that I love them. I hope not to use my kids as my excuse to achieve my goals; I want to equip them with a set of values that will give them true fullness of life.

I never imagined that a good life could come through all the tragedy we have been through, but it has. Although it hasn't been easy, it has been worth it.

I still struggle daily but I have learned to accept it and do my best to be positive. I have rejuvenated my passion for diet and exercise and can hardly go a day without it. Being in shape not only helps me physically but also mentally. Who would have ever guessed that it would take me losing my leg before I would become interested in running?

Forrest Gump said it best, "I just felt like running."

I have completed several 5ks and a half marathon using only forearm crutches. I have plans to complete a marathon soon. I am overwhelmed by the support I have received when I run. People will often stop me on the road to tell me how inspired they are. Some people even stop to offer me a ride. The look on their face is priceless when they realize I am running on purpose.

I used to be terrified of public speaking. I had a class in college where I had to give a presentation and my professor told me I was terrible. But as fate would have it, I ended up getting a job where I had to learn how to give presentations to an audience. Now I really enjoy public speaking. I have been blessed with many opportunities to share my story at churches, schools, events, retreats, and banquets. My hope is this book will give me more opportunities to share in the future.

I am truly thankful to all of those who have supported me through this journey. My hope is that this story was entertaining and inspiring and can help you in a kind of way.

Playing at LSU

Our wedding 2/8/2014

Barrett as a newborn

Me, David Joe and Tito December 27, 2018. The day before the accident

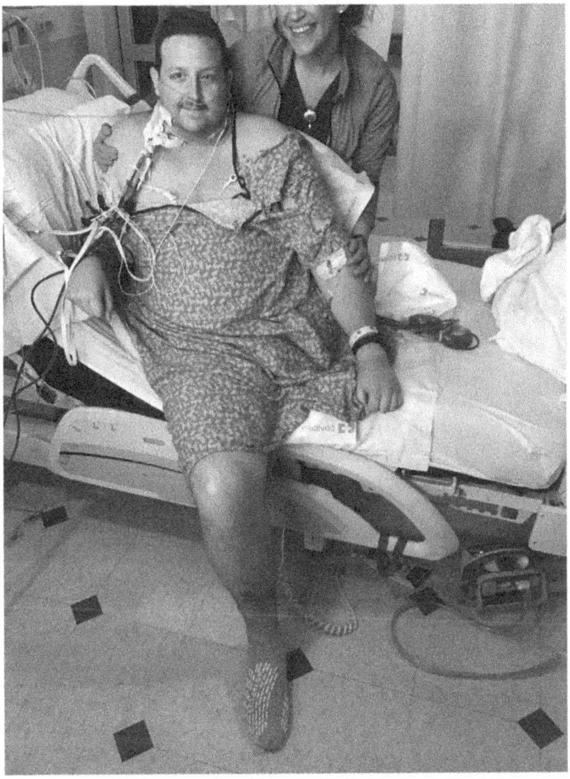

Day 21 in the ICU. The first time I was able to sit up enough to start the day on the right foot

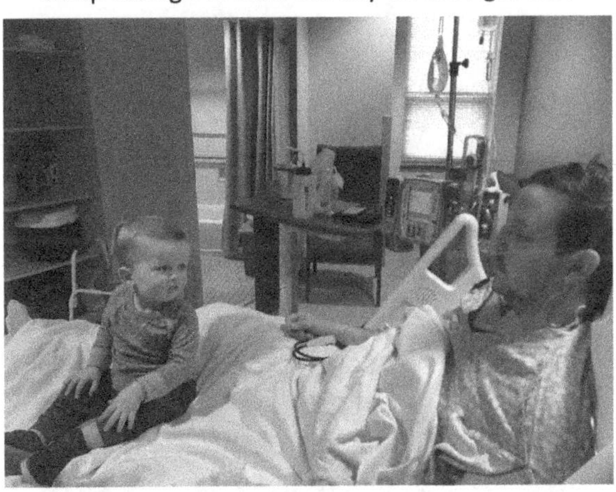

Barrett telling me to suck it up and come home already

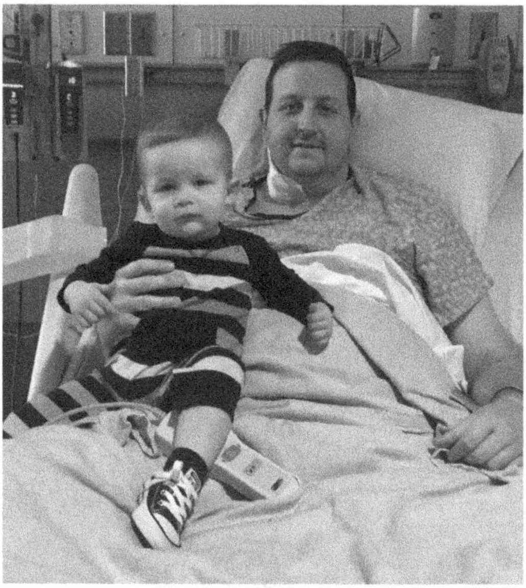

Father and son cheesing for the camera

Texas Turkey hunt after getting out of the hospital

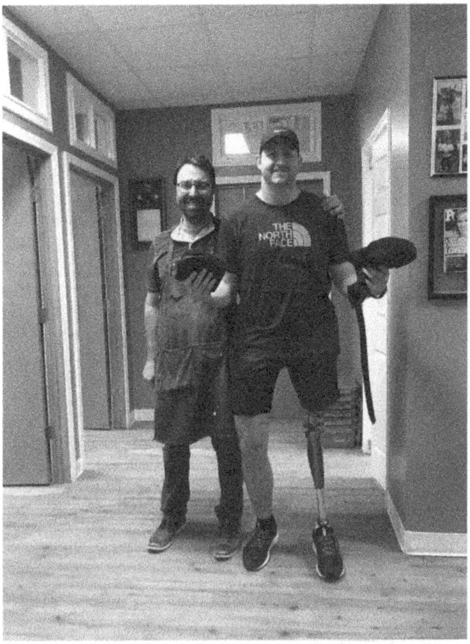

David sending me out with my prosthetic for the weekend

Our Navy Pier adventure

Matt Liana Barrett and Charlotte 2023

ACKNOWLEDGEMENTS

Liana- I would be lost without you. Thank you for being strong and giving me your best every day. You have a heart of gold and are a wonderful mother to Barrett and Charlotte. I will love you always.

Family- There are far too many of you to name but my hope is that each of you understands how important you are to me. I have received nothing but love and encouragement from each of you and I am forever grateful for that.

Friends- You all have stayed by my side and have never treated me differently because of my disability. I could not have gone through this without you.

Corteva Agriscience- My family and I have received unwavering emotional support and top-notch insurance coverage from this fabulous company. Everyone in the organization has been understanding and made sure I feel my needs are being taken care of. I could not have begun to put my life back together without your support.

David Rotter Prosthetics- You believed in me from the beginning of my journey. Your team's knowledge and expertise has helped me claim so much of my life back. I am forever grateful.

Writers- Kinny Haddox and Chase Turner, you were the first people I shared this book with. You gave me solid advice and confidence that it was worth publishing. Thank you!

LSU- Thank you for the opportunity to play football for the University. Although my career did not turn out like I hoped it would I can now say that my disappointing career served a greater purpose for me.

All Medical Staff- So many doctors and nurses at Merit Health River Region and University Mississippi Medical Center came together and allowed me to continue living life. I will be forever grateful for the passion and dedication each of you displays in the very important work that you do.

Community- To anyone who donated money, blood, time, or prayer. Our community has shown nothing but love and support for us through everything. Thank you!

Physics, Structure, and Reality